MW01519618

Series: *Language, Media & Education Studies*

Edited by: Marcel Danesi & Leonard G. Sbrocchi

1. M. Danesi, *Interpreting Advertisements. A Semiotic Guide*

2. M. Angenot, *Critique of Semiotic Reason*

3. S. Feigenbaum, *The Intermediate Sign in the System of French and Hebrew Verbs*

4. A. Bailin, *Metaphor and the Logic of Language Use*

5. C.D.E. Tolton, ed., *The Cinema of Jean Cocteau*

6. C. Madott Kosnik, *Primary Education: Goals, Processes and Practices*

7. F. Nuessel, *The Esperanto Language*

8. M.G. Guido, *The Acting Reader*

9. F. Ratto, *Hobbes tra scienza della politica e teoria delle passioni*

10. S. Battestini, *African Writing and Text*

11. T. A. Sebeok, *Essays in Semiotics I: Life Signs*

12. T. A. Sebeok, *Essays in Semiotics I: Culture Signs*

13. A. Ponzio and S. Petrilli, *Philosophy of Language, art and aswerability in Mikhail Baktin*

14. R. Beasley, M. Danesi, P. Perron, *Signs for Sale. An Outline of Semiotic Analysis for Advertisers & Marketers*

Ron Beasley, Marcel Danesi, Paul Perron

Signs for Sale

An outline of Semiotic Analysis for

Advertisers & Marketers

LEGAS

New York   Ottawa   Toronto

Canadian Cataloguing in Publication Data

Main entry under title:

Ron Beasley, Marcel Danesi, Paul Perron
>   *Signs for Sale*
>   *An Outline of Semiotic Analysis for Advertisers & Marketers*

(Language, media & education studies ; 14)
Includes bibliographical references
ISBN 1-894508-07-6

1. Advertising. 2. Semiotics. I. Danesi, Marcel, 1946-
II. Perron, Paul   III. Title.   IV. Series.

HF5822.B42 2000   659.1   C00900880-2

For further information and for orders:

LEGAS

P. O. Box 040328	68 Kamloops Ave.	2908 Dufferin Street
Brooklyn, New York	Ottawa, Ontario	Toronto, Ontario
USA 11204	K1V 7C9	M6B 3S8

Printed and bound in Canada

Contents

Preface..7

1. *Semiotics in Advertising*.............................9
    Advertising..11
    Semiotic Method.......................................13
    Semiotics in Advertising and Marketing.......................18
    Caveats..22
    Practical Activities
       (for Advertisers, Marketers, and Media Students)..............23

2. *Product Image*...25
    Brand Name and Logo...............................26
    Textuality...33
    The Use of Multiple Media.........................36
    Ad Campaigns..38
    Practical Activities
       (for Advertisers, Marketers, and Media Students)..............40

3. *Textuality*..43
    Generating Textuality..................................43
    The Connotative Index...............................47
    Verbal Techniques......................................50
    Nonverbal Techniques................................55
    Practical Activities
       (for Advertisers, Marketers, and Media Students)..............55

4. *Semiotically-Based Research*........................59
    Marketing Research....................................59
    Case Study 1...60
    Case Study 2...71
    Other Methods...76

Practical Activities
(for Advertisers, Marketers, and Media Students)........................78

5. *Synthesis and Concluding Thoughts*.................81

The Advertising Industry..82

Overview of Semiotic Method.....................................83

The Effects of Advertising..85

Practical Activities
(for Advertisers, Marketers, and Media Students)........................90

Glossary...95

Bibliography...99

Preface

To say that consumer product *advertising* has become the twentieth century's most ubiquitous means of mass communication is an understatement. The implicit messages, styles of presentation, and visual images of advertisers have become integral categories of the grammar of modern-day social discourse. They are found on all media of transmission —on posters, in magazines, in radio and TV commercials, on Internet sites, on pamphlets, on catalogues, and the list could go on and on. These are indelibly shaping the thoughts, personalities, and lifestyle behaviors of countless individuals, by tapping into the one need that distinguishes the human species from all others— the need for *meaning*.

The science that studies this need in all its manifestations is called *semiotics*. This manual is all about this science, focusing on its uses in the domain of advertising and marketing. It constitutes a highly modified second edition of a book published in the same series, titled *Interpreting Ads: A Semiotic Guide*, written by one of the authors of the present manual. The unexpected success of that book among the makers and promoters of advertising has led to the present volume, which, unlike *Interpreting Ads*, has been shaped to meet the specific request made by them for a "user-friendly" explication of the science that "advertisers have been probably practicing unknowingly all along," as one professional marketer put it to us recently. *Signs for Sale* has therefore been written as a manual explaining semiotic techniques to advertisers and marketers.

The manual is a collaboration of two academics and one marketing professional. It is based, in large part, on actual case studies in which the authors have been involved over the past decade. It is not a critical book about advertising, although it does reflect some of our views on the topic interspersed here and there. There are many excellent works currently on the market that look at the psychological and social implications of advertising that the reader can consult. Some of these are listed in the bibliography at the back. Nor is it designed to be a comprehensive, in-depth analysis of advertising methods. It is intended, simply, as a practical guide on how messages and meanings can be woven into, and extracted from, advertising texts. The approach employed, discussed, and illustrated throughout is intended to give only an initial glimpse into what semiotics has to offer to the profession of advertising. It can also be used in high school, college, and university courses preparing students for careers in advertising, marketing, and media.

Chapter 1 presents a brief historical overview of advertising and a condensed discussion of basic notions used in semiotics. Chapter 2 describes basic representational techniques that are used to generate a *product image*, as well as fundamental strategies for enhancing product recognizability through various media and ad campaigns. Chapter 3 deals with the ways in which ads and commercials generate *textuality*, as well as with the kinds of verbal and nonverbal techniques that are used to construct ads and commercials. Chapter 4 discusses and illustrates how semiotic ideas can be incorporated concretely into market research; it includes the description of two actual case studies in which the authors of this book have been involved. Chapter 5 provides a synthesis of semiotic ideas and contains our general reflections on the profession of advertising. Each chapter ends with a series of practical activities for classroom use. A convenient glossary of technical terms and a bibliography of suggested readings for more intensive study are included at the back.

We wish to thank the many advertisers, marketers, and companies who suggested to us that a "mini-course" in semiotics focusing on advertising as its target of application would be a very useful thing to have. There are too many to list here. We also wish to thank Victoria College of the University of Toronto, where one of the authors teaches and directs its Program in Semiotics and Communication Theory, for all the support that it has given to the serious study of semiotics over the years.

Ron Beasley, *ABM*
Marcel Danesi, *University of Toronto*
Paul Perron, *University of Toronto*

1. Semiotics in Advertising

The term *advertising* has come down to us from the medieval Latin verb *advertere* "to direct one's attention to." In line with its etymology, it can thus be defined as any type or form of public announcement intended to direct people's attention to the availability, qualities, and cost of specific commodities or services. Marketing research has made it obvious that products and services that are advertised, even in the simplest way through straightforward notification, have an advantage over those that are not in terms of saleability. This suggests a fundamental *Law of the Marketplace*—sales of a product are enhanced in relation to the amount of public exposure that it receives. The modern craft of advertising has, however, progressed considerably beyond the use of simple techniques for announcing the availability of products or services. It has ventured profitably into the domains of persuasion and entertainment. In the last fifty years, it is the persuasive, rhetorical form of advertising that has become a ubiquitous category of contemporary social discourse. Printed advertisements fill the pages of newspapers and magazines. Poster ads appear in buses, subways, trains, on city walls, etc. Neon signs along downtown streets flash consumeristic messages. Billboards dot the roadsides. Commercials interrupt TV and radio programs constantly. No wonder, then, that product names, logos, trademarks, sponsors, and the like have become household names and concepts. Having proven its effectiveness in the marketing of economic goods and services, since the early 1960s advertising has even been directed with increasing regularity towards matters of social concern. The ongoing cancer, anti-smoking, and antidrug abuse campaigns in North America are only three examples of the use of the advertising industry as a means to promote public welfare.

Today, advertising is definable as both an art and a science. It is an art because it employs aesthetic techniques designed to influence how people perceive goods and services. It is a science because it employs psychology and statistics to assess the effects of its techniques on consumer behavior; and this why it is closely linked with *marketing*. Advertisers and marketing agencies conduct extensive and expensive surveys to determine the potential acceptance of products or services before they are advertised at costs that may add up to millions of dollars. If the survey convinces the manufacturer that one of the versions exhibited will attract enough purchasers, a research crew then pretests various sales appeals by showing provisional advertisements to consumers and asking them to indicate their preference. After the one or two best-liked advertisements are identified, the advertiser produces a limited quantity of them and introduces them in a test market. On the basis of this test the advertiser-manufacturer can then make a decision as to whether a national campaign should be launched.

But advertising is only one of the modern-day means of enhancing the appeal of something or someone. Other common ones are the techniques of *propaganda, publicity,* and *public relations*:

- *Propaganda* is the craft of spreading and entrenching doctrines, views, beliefs, etc. reflecting specific interests and ideologies (political, social, philosophical, etc.).
- *Publicity* is the art of disseminating any information that concerns a person, group, event, or product through some public medium.
- *Public relations* is the profession employing activities and techniques designed to establish favorable attitudes and responses towards organizations, institutions, and/or individuals on the part of the general public or special groups.

Advertising falls into two main categories: (1) *consumer advertising*, which is directed towards the promotion of some product or service to the general public (or market segment thereof), and (2) *trade advertising*, which is directed to dealers and professionals through appropriate trade publications and media. The focus of this book is on the former, which can be defined more specifically as any announcement designed to promote the sale of marketable goods and services. Consumer advertising gave birth to the first agency for recording and analyzing data on advertising effectiveness in 1914 with the establishment of the *Audit Bureau of Circulations* in the United States, an independent organization founded and supported by newspaper and magazine publishers wishing to obtain circulation statistics and to standardize the ways of presenting them. Then, in 1936, the *Advertising Research Foundation* was established to conduct research on, and to develop, advertising techniques with the capacity to enhance the authenticity, reliability, efficiency, and usefulness of all advertising and marketing research. Today, the increasing sophistication with statistical information-gathering techniques makes it possible for advertisers to target audiences on the basis of where people live, what income they make, what educational background they have, etc. in order to determine their susceptibility to, or inclination towards, certain products.

Advertising

Most historians believe that outdoor signs displayed above the shop doors of several ancient cities of the Middle East were the first advertising artifacts of human civilization. As early as 3000 BC, the Babylonians, who lived in what is now Iraq, used such signs to advertise the stores themselves. The ancient Greeks and Romans also hung signs outside their shops. Since few people could read, merchants of the era used recognizable symbols carved in stone, clay, or wood for their signs. A poster found in Thebes in 1000 BC is a relic of one of the world's first print ads. In large letters, it offered a whole gold coin for the capture of a runaway slave. Archeologists have found similar kinds of posters scattered all over ancient societies. Throughout history, poster advertising in marketplaces and temples has, in fact, constituted a popular means of disseminating information and of promoting the barter and sale of goods. In medieval times, in addition to print advertising, word-of-mouth praise of products by so-called town criers was also used to great advantage.

The technological event that made print the most common form of advertising, until the advent of electronic media in the twentieth century, occurred in the fifteenth century when the printed word was made available to masses of people through the invention of the modern printing press by Johann Gutenberg (1400?-1468). Fliers and posters could be printed easily and posted in public places or inserted in books, pamphlets, newspapers, etc. In the latter part of the seventeenth century, the *London Gazette* became the first newspaper to reserve a section exclusively for advertising. So successful was this venture that by the end of the century new agencies came into being for the specific purpose of creating newspaper ads for merchants, artisans, etc. Print advertising spread even more rapidly throughout the eighteenth century. This led to the establishment of the first advertising agency by Philadelphia entrepreneur Volney B. Palmer in 1841. By 1849, Palmer had offices in New York, Boston, and Baltimore in addition to his Philadelphia office. In the first decades of the twentieth century, the increased use of electricity led to the illuminated outdoor poster; and photoengraving and other printing inventions helped both the editorial and advertising departments of printed journals create truly effective texts.

Between 1890 and 1920 industrial corporations grew into mammoth structures that transformed the workplace into an integrated economic system of mass production. It was at that point in time that advertising came to be perceived primarily as an instrument of persuasion by corporate executives. Business and aesthetics had joined forces by the first decades of the twentieth century. From the 1920s onwards, advertising agencies sprang up all over, broadening their attempts to build an unbroken, imagistic bridge between the product and the consumer's consciousness. Everything from product name, design, and packaging came gradually within the purview of the advertising business. The advent of radio, also in the 1920s, led to the invention of a new form of advertising, known as the *commercial*—a mini-narrative or drama revolving around a product and its uses, which became highly influential as a vehicle of persuasion with the advent of television in the late 1940s and early 1950s. TV commercials of the day, such as *Folger* coffee's pseudoscientific sales pitches, *Mum* deodorant's satires of spy movies, and *Pepsodent* toothpaste's animations with snappy jingles, became so familiar that perception of the product became inextricably intertwined with the content of its commercial. The commercial also created the first advertising personalities, from *Mr. Clean* (representing a detergent product of the same name) to *Speedy* (a personified *Alka-Seltzer* tablet) —and became a source of the dissemination of recognizable tunes throughout society— from *Mr. Clean in a just a minute* (for the *Mr. Clean* detergent product) to *Plop, plop, fizz, fizz oh what a relief it is* (for the *Alka-Seltzer* stomach product). Recently, the Internet has come forward to complement and supplement both the *print* and *commercial* (radio and TV) forms of advertising.

Today, advertising has established itself as one of the most pervasive forms of social communication. Manufacturers advertise to persuade people to buy their products. Business firms, political parties and candidates, social organizations, special-interest groups, and the government advertise to create a favorable "image" of themselves. Advertising has developed into a privileged form of social discourse that has displaced, by and large, more traditional forms —sermons, political oratory, proverbs, wise sayings, etc.— which in previous centuries had unchallenged rhetorical force and moral authority. The categories of this discourse are, however, highly ephemeral and vacuous. This is, of course, intentional. The inbuilt ephemerality of advertising makes it possible to:

- ensure that newness and faddishness can be reflected in the product through adaptive change in the style and content of ads and commercials;
- ensure that any changes in social trends (fashion, music, values, popularity of media personalities, etc.) also be reflected in ads and commercials;
- ensure that the product's identity keep in step with the times;
- ensure that the consumer's changing needs and perceptions be built into the textuality (form and content) of ads and commercials, thus creating a dynamic interplay between advertising and social lifestyle, whereby one influences the other through a constant synergy.

Given the obvious influence of advertising on the development of modern culture, the French semiotician Roland Barthes (1915-1980) drew attention in the 1950s to the value of studying its messages and techniques with the theoretical tools of the science of *semiotics*. After the publication of his pivotal book *Mythologies* in 1957, a new branch of research in semiotics sprang up, focusing on how advertising generates its meanings, animating, at the same time, a society-wide debate on the broader ethical and spiritual questions raised by the entrenchment of advertising as a form of aesthetics and entertainment in the mindset of contemporary society. Particularly worrisome to Barthes was the fact that the constant change in advertising styles, techniques, and modes of delivery tended to create an incessant craving for new goods. He called this culturally induced state of mind "neomania," which he defined simply as an obsessive desire for new objects of consumption. Barthes also criticized caustically the fact that advertising proposes marketplace solutions to social problems, elevating shopping to much more than just acquiring the essentials required for daily living. As O'Neill-Karch (2000, pp. 11-12) points out, one advertising campaign, the *Absolut Vodka* one of the 1980s and 1990s, even went so far as to imbue its product with the spiritual qualities that are perceived to be so lacking in the hubris of modern society. It started with a bottle shown with a halo and the caption *Absolut Perfection*; it then progressed to a winged bottle with the caption *Absolut Heaven*; and, more recently, to a bottle held by the hand of a medieval knight with the caption *Absolut Grail* (in medieval legend the grail was the plate or cup from which Christ drank at the Last Supper and which Joseph of Arimathea used to receive the blood from the wounds of the crucified Christ). The overall message of the campaign was rather transparent— namely, that spirituality could be obtained by imbibing the vodka.

Semiotic Method

Modern-day semiotic method is based on the writings of the American logician Charles S. Peirce (1839-1914) and the French linguist Ferdinand de Saussure (1857-1913). The reason why semiotics lends itself well, not only to the critique of advertising, but also as a source of insight into the making of advertisements and commercials, is because it provides the theoretical tools, developed largely by Saussure and Peirce, for understanding how we encode and decode meaning from the many *representations* we make.

For the sake of historical accuracy, it should be mentioned that semiotics grew out of the study by the ancient physicians of the Western world of the physiological symptoms produced by particular diseases. The term *semiotics* (spelled originally *semeiotics*), from Greek *semeion* "mark, sign," was coined by the founder of Western medical science, Hippocrates (460-377 BC). A *symptom* is, in fact, a perfect example of what a *semeion* is. It is a noticeable sign—a dark bruise, a rash, a sore throat, etc.—that stands for some physical condition—a broken finger, a skin allergy, a cold, etc.

Symptom

something noticeable	standing for	something else
⇓		⇓
a dark bruise		a broken finger
a rash		a skin allergy
a sore throat		a cold

Medical science is, in effect, basic semiotic science, since it is grounded on the principle that the symptom is a trace to an inner state, condition, etc. The fundamental thing to notice about the *semeion* is that its consists of two parts, the discernible symptom itself and the probable condition it indicates. The two are inseparable: i.e. there is no symptom that is not caused by some bodily condition, and, vice versa, there is no condition that does not produce symptoms (detectable or not). The *semeion* is a *natural sign*, i.e. a sign produced by Nature. But humans have also produced their own signs —e.g. words, gestures, symbols, etc.— that can stand for things other than bodily conditions. These are called *conventional signs*, since they are invented by human beings in cultural settings for conventionalized purposes. Like natural signs, they also consist of two parts: (1) a physical part —e.g. the sounds or letters that make up a word such as *cat*— and, (2) the entity, object, being, event, etc. that the physical part has been designed to stand for, whether it be real or imagined:

Conventional Sign

something perceivable	standing for	something real or imagined
⇓		⇓
cat (= three perceivable sounds joined together)		

The above is an example of a *concrete sign*, i.e. of a sign that stands for something that can be demonstrated or perceived directly with the senses. But conventional signs can also refer to *abstract* things, i.e. to things that exist only in the mind and cannot be demonstrated directly. As an example of an abstract sign, observe the following figure.

The meaning of this sign as a "bright idea" requires some "figuring out" and background culture knowledge. A lit *light bulb* illuminates a situation —hence the designation "bright." The *balloon* figure, which contains the light bulb, is found commonly in cartoon strips and comics to represent something inside the mind— hence the designation "idea." The meaning of "bright idea" associated with this sign is based historically on the fact that we associate *light* and *knowledge* with each other in our culture. This is why we say such things as the following:

1. That is a *brilliant* idea.
2. His ideas are *illuminating*.
3. I saw what he said in the *light* of reason.
4. His ideas have shed *light* on many things.
5. She is living in the *dark ages*.
6. The *Enlightenment* was an important movement in the intellectual development of Western culture.
7. There is *light* at the end of the tunnel.

Incidentally, the "bright idea" figure above is classified as a *nonverbal sign*; words and other linguistic structures (expressions, phrases, etc.) are classified instead as *verbal signs*. Conventional signs serve a fundamental need in human cognitive life. They allow humans to remember the world. Knowing and using words like *cat* and figures like the one above allow people to recognize the same things over and over in all kinds of situations. Without signs we would have to experience things and represent them anew each time we came across them or each time we imagined them. Signs are found in all forms of representation and communication. They make thinking and communication fluid and routine.

The diagnosis of a sore throat can be used to show how semioticians (not to mention doctors) go about conducting their investigations. First, the semiotician would see it instantly as a *semeion*, because it is something physically discernible standing for something other than itself. The particular term used to designate the physical part of the sign itself —which in this case is characterizable as an observable "redness" producing an appreciable soreness— is the *signifier*. The term *representamen* is sometimes used in semiotic theory in lieu of *signifier*. We will use only *signifier* in this book. Next, the semiotician would consider the *context* or location of the signifier (in this case the throat). This determines, or at least constrains, the particular meaning that it entails— soreness in other parts of the body would, in fact, indicate a different medical analysis. This is called its *signified*. The words *referent* and *object* are often used as synonyms for *signified* in the semiotic literature. We will use mainly *signified* in this book. In this case, the signified is a "sore throat." Finally, the connection of this meaning to what it implies medically is called *signification*. Through previous experience, doctors can safely predict, in most cases, that sore throats are caused by such conditions as colds, infections, etc. The term *interpretation* is sometimes used instead of *signification* — although this has many other meanings in semiotics.

The same method of inquiry is used to study conventional signs. In effect, semiotic analysis consists in establishing *signification* relations between *signifiers* and *signifieds* by asking questions such as the following:

- Who or what created the sign?
- What does it mean?
- How does it deliver its meaning?
- What medium (verbal, nonverbal, etc.) was employed?
- For whom was it intended, or how did it come about?
- In what context does it occur?
- To what system of signification does it belong?
- How many interpretations are possible under the circumstances?

Semiotics is to be differentiated from what has come to be known in the last fifty years as *communication science*. Although the two share much of the same conceptual and methodological territory, communication scientists generally focus more on the technical study of how messages are transmitted (vocally, electronically, etc.), whereas semioticians center their attention more on what a message means and on how it creates meaning.

The fact that human-made signs bear their meanings through social and historical *convention* was first pointed out by Aristotle (384-322 BC) and the Stoic philosophers (a Greek school of philosophy, founded by Zeno around 308 BC). A little later, it was St. Augustine (354-430 AD), the philosopher and religious thinker, who distinguished between the signs found in Nature as *natural* —the colors of leaves, the shape of plants, the physiology of symptoms, etc.— and those made by humans —words, symbols, figures, etc.— as *conventional*. St. Augustine also proposed that in every human sign there exists an implicit *interpretive* dimension that constrains its meaning. This was consistent with the so-called *hermeneutic* tradition established earlier by Clement of Alexandria (150?-215? AD), the Greek theologian and early Father of the Church. *Hermeneutics* is the study and interpretation of ancient texts, especially those of a religious or mythical nature. Today, it is a branch of semiotics aiming to study how all texts generate meaning. The idea is to establish, as far as possible, the meaning that a text entails on the basis of symbolic considerations, relevant sources, and historical background. Incidentally, for the sake of historical accuracy, the Saussurean notions mentioned above are actually traceable to the medieval Scholastic tradition — a philosophical movement that was dominant in the medieval Christian schools and universities of Europe from about the middle of the eleventh century to about the middle of the fifteenth century. The Scholastics defined the sign as "something that stands for something else," made up of two parts, the *signans* (= signifier), defined as something perceptible by the senses, and the *signatum* (= signified), defined as the idea, object, event, etc. to which the sign refers.

John Locke (1632-1704), the English philosopher who set out the principles of empiricism, introduced the formal study of signs into philosophy in his *Essay Concerning Human Understanding* (1690), anticipating that it would allow philosophers to understand the interconnection between representation and knowledge. But the task he laid out remained virtually unnoticed until, as mentioned above, the ideas of the Swiss linguist Ferdinand de Saussure and the American philosopher Charles S. Peirce became the basis for circumscribing an autonomous field of inquiry. In his *Cours de linguistique générale* (1916), a textbook put together after his death by two of his university students, Saussure used the term *semiology* to designate the field he proposed for studying these structures. But while his term is still used somewhat today, the older term *semiotics* is the preferred one. Saussure emphasized that the study of signs should be divided into two branches — the *synchronic* and the *diachronic*. The former refers to the study of signs at a given point in time, normally the present, and the latter to the investigation of how signs change in form and meaning over time. A large part of the increase in the popularity of the field in the late twentieth century was brought about by the popular fictional writings of Umberto Eco (1932-), a leading practitioner of semiotics. The success of his best-selling novels (*The Name of the Rose, Foucault's Pendulum, The Island of the Day Before*) has stimulated considerable curiosity vis-à-vis semiotics in recent years among the public at large. The work of Thomas A. Sebeok (1920-), a distinguished professor of semiotics at Indiana University, has also been instrumental in showing the relevance of semiotics to those working in cognate disciplines. Sebeok has frequently compared semiotics to a spider's web, because it rarely fails to entrap scientists, educators, and humanists into its intricate loom of insights into human representation.

The premise that guides semiotic analysis is that the recurring patterns that characterize sign systems are reflective of innate *structures* in the sensory, emotional, and intellectual composition of the human body and the human psyche — hence the term *structuralism* in the literature to refer to semiotic method. This would explain why the forms of expression that humans create and to which they respond instinctively the world over are so meaningful and so easily understandable across cultures. For the sake of accuracy, it should also be mentioned that, in recent years, a *post-structuralist* school of thought has emerged within semiotics, receiving some attention, especially among the users of semiotic theory (e.g. literary critics, educators, etc.). The leading figure of this school is the French semiotician and philosopher Jacques Derrida (1930-). The main premise in post-structuralism is that signs and texts have a constantly changing meaning. But post-structuralism has produced very few useable results in reforming basic semiotic method. Its most beneficial effect on semiotics has been to make analysts more aware of the subjectivity that interpretation invariably entails.

Semiotics in Advertising and Marketing

Advertising is all about *signification* through skillful *representation*. The fundamental *Law of Marketing* alluded to above can, in fact, be rephrased semiotically as follows — the saleability of a product or service correlates with the effectiveness of an ad or commercial to link the product or service conceptually with some desire or need (erotic, social power, attractiveness, family happiness, etc.) through some culturally-significant *representational* process. The process often involves associating a product with a critical social event or ritual.

Consider, for instance, the following ad for *Russell and Bromley* shoes that was popular a few years ago in magazines:

A semiotic analysis of this ad is guided by a series of leading questions, such as the following three:

- Question 1: *What are the observable features of the ad that stand out? (= What are the signifiers of the ad?)*

- A young woman has just walked through a portal.
- She has her eyes closed and her expression seems to convey a kind of sensual rapture.
- She is wearing a white dress, contrasting with her dark hair.
- Her pumps are white, but the tips are black and they are pointing "downwards."
- She is sitting on a staircase that is leading downwards.
- She has her hands between her thighs.
- The folds of her dress make a V-shaped design, as does the positioning of her arms and, in an inverted way, the contour of her legs.

- Question 2: *What does each one suggest? (= What are the signifieds that may be associated with the above signifiers?)*

- Walking through a portal indicates, generally, a passage rite, which, in this case, is suggestive of a coming-of-age rite, given that the wearing of sexually suggestive clothing and shoes is typical of such rites throughout the world.
- The contrast between white and black is suggestive of a contrast between innocence and sexuality (maturity).
- The pointing downwards of the shoes suggests a descent into an "underworld" of desire and sexual ecstasy, feelings that emerge at maturity. This signified is reinforced by the staircase that only leads down.
- The position of the young woman's hands and the V-shape of the dress folds, of her arms and legs, are suggestive of female genitalia.

Question 3: *What overall theme does the ad suggest? (= What signification/interpretation can be assigned to the ad?)*

The way in which this ad has been put together is strongly suggestive of a coming-of-age rite involving a "sexualization" of the body through appropriate clothing. Pumps in particular are symbols (signifiers) of sexuality for females. But semioticians would not stop at this fairly straightforward analysis of the ad. They would, in fact, go one step further. The "underworld" has a long-standing sexual-erotic meaning in Western mythology. The *Russell & Bromley* ad is, in a representational sense, a modern-day advertiser's version of the myth of Persephone, the Greek goddess of fertility and queen of the underworld. Persephone was the daughter of Zeus and Demeter. When she was still a beautiful maiden, Pluto seized her and held her captive in his underworld. Though Demeter eventually persuaded the gods to let her daughter return to her, Persephone was required to remain in the underworld for four months because Pluto had tricked her into eating a pomegranate (food of the dead) there. When Persephone left the earth, the flowers withered and the grain died, but when she returned, life blossomed anew.

But this is not the only myth that could have been enlisted to make sense of the particular way in which the ad text was put together. The myth of Orpheus and Eurydice is another one that could have been similarly utilized. It is not important that one or the other mythical *interpretation* of the ad is the correct one; what counts is that a mythical interpretation was possible in the first place. In fact, the more interpretations there are, the more likely the effectiveness of the ad (as will be discussed in subsequent chapters). This suggests a corollary to the fundamental *Law of the Marketplace* enunciated above — namely, that the effectiveness of an ad varies according to the suggestive images it generates; the more suggestive, the more effective, thus enhancing product saleability.

A perceptive definition of *semiotics* that is relevant to the foregoing discussion has been put forward by Umberto Eco himself in his 1976 book *A Theory of Semiotics*. Eco defines semiotics as: "the discipline studying everything which can be used in order to lie," because if "something cannot be used to tell a lie, conversely it cannot be used to tell the truth; it cannot, in fact, be used to tell at all" (p. 7). This is, despite its apparent facetiousness, a rather insightful definition, since it implies that we have the capacity to represent the world in any way we desire through signs, even in misleading and deceitful ways. This capacity for representational artifice is a powerful one indeed. It allows us to conjure up nonexistent concepts, or refer to the world without any back-up empirical proof that what we are saying is true.

Following Eco, modern-day advertising can be defined as the art of persuasion through representational artifice. This can take many forms and manifest itself in many ways. Common representational ploys used by advertisers include:

- the something-for-nothing lure (*Buy one and get a second one free! Send for free sample! Trial offer at half price! No money down!* etc.);
- the use of humor to generate a feeling of pleasantness towards a product;
- endorsement by celebrities to make a product appear reliable;
- inducing parents to believe that giving their children certain products will secure them a better life and future;

- appealing to children to "ask mummy or daddy" to buy certain products, thus increasing the likelihood that parents will "give in" to their children's requests;

- using *scare copy* techniques designed to promote such goods and services as insurance, fire alarms, cosmetics, and vitamin capsules by evoking the fear of poverty, sickness, loss of social standing, and/or impending disaster;

- and, of course, creating ads and commercials that are highly suggestive of erotic, sensual, mythic, and other kinds of psychologically powerful themes (as we saw above).

These techniques have become so intrinsic to the art of advertising that they are no longer recognized consciously as representational stratagems. Advertising has become, in effect, an integral component of an entertainment-driven society that seeks artifice as part of its routine of escapism from the deeper philosophical questions that would otherwise beset it. Advertising is powerful because it offers the hope of more money and better jobs, security against the hazards of old age and illness, popularity and personal prestige, praise from others, more comfort, increased enjoyment, social advancement, improved appearance, better health, erotic stimulation, and so on. The effectiveness of the techniques used to generate such messages is limited only by the ingenuity of the advertiser, by the limits of the various channels of communication, by certain legal restrictions, and by standards self-imposed by the advertising industry.

Caveats

There are three caveats that must be stated clearly from the very outset. First, the degree to which an ad, such as the above *Russell & Bromley* ad, will induce consumers to buy the manufacturer's product is an open question. In any case, it is certainly not the point of semiotic analysis to determine this. Simply put, the *Russell & Bromley* ad is effective *representationally*; in our view it is effective *psychologically* only to the degree to which consumers can identify with its implicit sexually charged coming-of-age theme. Nor is it the goal of semiotics to criticize makers of such ads. On the contrary, semioticians should, in theory, approach an ad like they would a work of art. The same questions that art and literary critics ask about a painting or a novel are the ones that a semiotician should ask about an ad. To the semiotician, advertising provides an opportunity to examine how varied aesthetic experiences and classical forms of expression are realized in a contemporary medium

A second caveat to be expressed from the outset is that the interpretation of any ad (sometimes called *decoding*) is just that — one possible interpretation. Indeed, disagreement about what something means is not only unavoidable, but also part of the fun of doing semiotics. Differences of opinion fill the pages of the semiotic research journals and lead, as in other sciences, to a furthering of knowledge in the field. The point of this manual is simply to display the techniques of semiotic analysis, not to provide a series of critical interpretations of ads and commercials. In this way, our hope is that the appetite of advertisers and marketers will be whetted just enough for them to pursue a more in-depth study of semiotics and, perhaps, to consider critically what they are doing.

A third caveat is that semiotics is not a branch of advertising or marketing. It is an autonomous science that aims to investigate *semiosis*—the capacity to produce and comprehend signs—and *representation*—the activity of using signs to make messages and meanings. Advertising agencies have rarely, as far as we can surmise, sought the aid of semiotics in carrying out their creative activities, including ad style, graphic design, copy writing, print and broadcast production, and research to study audience reaction and response.

Practical Activities
(for Advertisers, Marketers, and Media Students)

1. In line with the *Law of the Marketplace* suggest strategies for enhancing product recognizability.

2. What aspects of modern-day large businesses entail *propaganda, publicity,* and *public relations,* in addition to *advertising* and/or *marketing*?

3. Can you think of ways, other than those mentioned in this chapter that can ensure that a product will "generate new demand" continually?

4. Can you add to *Absolut Vodka's* "spirituality ad campaign," suggesting other ways of presenting the product in print ads?

5. For the following signs, some of which are product names, only the *signifiers* are given. Provide their *signifieds* and what they mean overall in cultural terms (*signification*).

Signifier	Signified	Signification
Gucci		
Macintosh		
☜		
⇒		
⇐		
r		
Z		
Camels		
Marlboros		
Budweiser		
Heineken		

6. Suggest ways of updating the *Russell & Bromley* ad to meet contemporary fashion, and body image (including hairstyle) standards. Design your own ad, changing the mythic narrative.

2. Product Image

Three primary strategies are used commonly today to enhance product recognizability, in line with the *Law of the Marketplace* mentioned in the previous chapter. These are known generally as *repetition, positioning*, and the creation of an *image* for the product. *Repetition* is a basic marketing technique. A typical national advertiser can capture the attention of prospective customers by repeated appeals to buy some product through sales talks on radio and television, advertisements for the same product in newspapers and magazines, and poster displays in stores and elsewhere (on subway panels, buses, etc.). *Positioning* is the targeting of a product through appropriate advertising for the right audience of consumers—e.g. the *Russell & Bromley* accessories (shoes and purses) are positioned for a female audience of a certain social class, *Nike* shoes for a trendy adolescent and young adult audience; *Audis* and *BMWs* are positioned for an up-scale class of consumers, *Dodge vans* for a middle-class suburban one; and so on. Positioning is likewise a fundamental marketing strategy. The creation of an *image* for a product can be described as a particular configuration of signifieds built into a product that renders it appealing to specific types of consumers. *Budweiser* beer, for instance, evokes the image of "ruggedness" and "athletics," whereas *Heineken* evokes an image of "smoothness" and "sophistication." This is why commercials for *Budweiser* are positioned next to sports events on television, and why those for *Heineken* are found primarily in "high brow" magazines.

An *image* is, clearly, constructed on the basis of socially based *representation*. This can be defined simply as the art of constructing a *signification system* for a product. For example, the *State Farm* insurance company has established such a system for itself through the use of four main representational techniques: (1) a brand name (*State Farm*) that can be associated with "down-to-earth" (agrarian, country, rural) values, especially friendliness and trustworthiness; (2) a logo (outreaching hands) that communicates the same signifieds; (3) a jingle (*Like a good neighbor, State Farm is there*) that reiterates and reinforces the signifieds; (4) ads and commercials portraying *State Farm* employees as wholesome, neighborly individuals ready to help out in time of need. From this signification system an *image* of the *State Farm* company as a "friendly" and "trustworthy" institution has crystallized over the years, becoming fixed in the social mindset through repeated advertising campaigns.

This chapter has two objectives: (1) to briefly describe some of the basic representational techniques that are used to generate signification systems for products and services; and (2) to discuss how recognizability and image are established through various media and ad campaigns. Needless to say, it is impossible to go into any depth or detail here. The reader interested in getting a broader treatment of representational theory, for instance, can consult the suggested readings in semiotics at the back. These will help fill-in the gaps left by the present treatment.

Brand Name and Logo

To say that a product has a certain image or evokes a system of *meaning*, implies that it has been represented in a regular way to convey that image. In advertising and semiotics, the word *meaning* comes up continually. But what does meaning *mean*? Consider the following vignette devised by Hayakawa (1991: 91), which shows how people become entangled in logical circularities when asked to define something:

- What do you mean by democracy?
- *Democracy means the preservation of human rights.*
- What do you mean by rights?
- *I mean those privileges God grants all of us—I mean man's inherent privileges.*
- Such as?
- *Liberty, for example.*
- What do you mean by liberty?
- *Religious and political freedom.*
- And what does that mean?
- *Religious and political freedom is what we enjoy under a democracy.*

Explaining the meaning of concepts such as *democracy* not only leads to logical entanglements, but, as the psychologist C. K. Ogden and the philosopher and literary critic I. A. Richards showed in their classic 1923 work, titled appropriately *The Meaning of Meaning*, the word *meaning* itself has many *meanings*. Here are some of them:

He *means* to write	=	"intends"
A green light *means* go	=	"indicates"
Health *means* everything	=	"has importance"
Her look was full of *meaning*	=	"special import"
Does life have a *meaning*?	=	"purpose"
What does love *mean* to you?	=	"convey"

In effect, the term *meaning* defies definition. Like the basic axioms of Euclidean geometry, it is best left as a notion of which everyone has an intuitive understanding, but which cannot itself be explained in absolute terms. It is a semiotic *given*. The term *signification*, as we saw in the previous chapter, is much easier to define, even though *meaning* and *signification* are often used interchangeably by many semioticians. Essentially, *signification* designates the particular thoughts and responses that a sign evokes. *Signification* is not an open-ended process, however; it is constrained by a series of factors, including conventional agreements as to what a sign means in specific contexts, the type of *code* to which it belongs, the nature of its referents —concrete referents are less subject to variation than are abstract ones— and so on. Without such inbuilt constraints, signification and communication would be virtually impossible in common social settings.

The basic strategy used in creating a *signification system* for a product is *brand naming*. At a practical level, naming a product has a *denotative* function, i.e. it allows consumers to identify what product they desire to purchase (or not). Consider the name given to the pumps —*Russell & Bromley*— discussed in the previous chapter. Denotatively, the name allows us to identify the shoes, should we desire to buy them. However, this is not all it does. The use of the manufacturer's name, rather than some invented name or expression, assigns an aura of artistry, craftsmanship, and superior quality to the product. The shoes can thus be perceived to be the "work" of an artist (the manufacturer). They constitute a "work of shoe art," so to speak, not just an assembly-line product for everyone to wear. This is a widely used strategy in the area of advertising for lifestyle products. In the fashion industry, *designer* names such as *Armani, Gucci,* and *Calvin Klein* evoke images of *objets d'art*, rather than images of mere clothes, shoes, or jewelry; so too do names such as *Ferrari, Lamborghini,* and *Maserati* in the domain of automobiles. The manufacturer's name, in such cases, *extends* the denotative meaning of the product considerably. This extensional process is known as *connotation*. The signification system created to ensconce product image into the social mindset is a *de facto* connotative one. When people buy an *Armani* or a *Gucci* product, for instance, they feel that they are buying a painting, a sculpture, a work of art to be displayed on the body; when they buy *Poison*, by *Christian Dior*, they sense that they are buying a dangerous, but alluring, love potion; when they buy *Moondrops, Natural Wonder, Rainflower, Sunsilk,* or *Skin Dew* cosmetics they feel that they are acquiring some of Nature's beauty resources; and when they buy *Eterna 27, Clinique, Endocil,* or *Equalia* beauty products they sense that they are getting products imbued with scientific validity. *No-name* products do not engender such systems of connotations.

The connotations of "sexuality" and "maturity," as we saw in the previous chapter, are also part of the signification system that the *Russell & Bromley* shoes evoke. These derive from the fact that *high heel* shoes are perceived as sexy and, thus, to be worn only by mature women (not preadolescent girls). At a denotative level a *shoe* can be defined simply as "a durable covering for the human foot." It is something that makes locomotion much more endurable than walking barefoot. This denotative signified can be seen in utterances such as: "I bought a new pair of *shoes* yesterday;" "*Shoe* prices are continually going up in this city;" "We threw out our old *shoes* the other day;" and so on. But, by connotative extension, the *type* of shoes one wears carries along with it certain *social connotations*. High heel shoes have a long history of association with eroticism. This is why we talk of *shoe fetishes* and why erotic depictions of females seem to be more sexually enticing when high heel shoes are worn than when they are not. Thus, wearing *Russell & Bromley* high heel shoes entails, more precisely, wearing "a work of erotic shoe art."

The overall configuration of the above signifieds creates a signification system for the *Russell & Bromley* product that can be schematized as follows:

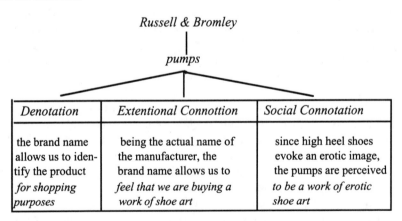

Denotation	Extentional Connottion	Social Connotation
the brand name allows us to identify the product *for shopping purposes*	being the actual name of the manufacturer, the brand name allows us to *feel that we are buying a work of shoe art*	since high heel shoes evoke an erotic image, the pumps are perceived *to be a work of erotic shoe art*

Incidentally, *branding* was, originally, the searing of flesh with a hot iron to produce a scar or *mark* with an easily recognizable pattern for identification or other purposes. Livestock were branded by the Egyptians as early as 2000 BC. In the late medieval period, trades people and guild members posted characteristic *marks* outside their shops, leading to the notion of *trademark*. Medieval swords and ancient Chinese pottery, for instance, were also marked with identifiable symbols so buyers could trace their origin and determine their quality. Among the best-known trademarks surviving from early modern times are the striped pole of the barbershop and the three-ball sign of the pawnbroker shop. Names were first used towards the end of the nineteenth century when many American firms began to market packaged goods under brand names. Previously, everyday household products were sold in neighborhood stores from large bulk containers. Around 1880, soap manufacturers started *naming* their products so that they could be identified. The first modern-day *brand names* were thus invented. They included: *Ivory, Pears', Sapolio, Colgate, Kirk's American Family*, and *Packer's*. Soon afterward, other manufacturers joined the bandwagon, adding names such as *Royal Baking Powder, Quaker Oats, Baker's Chocolate, Hire's Root Beer, Regal Shoes, Waterman's Pens, Bon Ami, Wrigley, and Coca-Cola* to the growing list of products that were being identified with *brand names*.

Trademarks are the pictorial counterparts of brand names. Known also as *logos* (an abbreviation of *logogriphs*), they are used to generate the same kinds of connotative signification systems for a product, typically in a complementary fashion. Consider the *McDonald's* golden arches logo as a case-in-point. The arches seem to beckon good people to march through them triumphantly into a paradise of Puritan values — law and order, cleanliness, friendliness, hospitality, hard work, self-discipline, and family values. Like the arches of ancient cities, they symbolize tradition and allegiance. From the menu to the uniforms, *McDonald's* exacts and imposes standardization, in the same way that the world's organized religions do. As any ritualistic experience, the eating event at *McDonald's* is designed to be socially functional. Fewer and fewer North Americans have the time to eat meals together within the household, let alone the energy to prepare elaborate dinners. In modern-day households, meals are routinely consumed in front of television sets. The home, ironically, has become a place where people now tend to eat apart. Enter *McDonald's* to the rescue! In the cheery atmosphere of a *McDonald's* restaurant, family members can be brought together, at the same table, under the same roof.

As one other example, consider the apple logo adopted by the *Apple* computer company. This, too, is charged with latent religious connotations, suggesting the story of Adam and Eve in the Western Bible, which revolves around the eating of an apple that was supposed to contain secret forbidden knowledge. In actual fact, the Hebrew account of the Genesis story tells of a "forbidden" fruit, not specifically of an apple. The representation of this fruit as an apple came about in medieval depictions of the Eden scene, when painters and sculptors became interested in the Genesis story artistically. In the Koran, on the other hand, the forbidden fruit is a banana. Now, the Biblical symbolism of the apple as "forbidden knowledge" continues to resonate in our culture. This is why the *Apple* computer company has not only named itself with the word *Apple*, but has also chosen the picture of this fruit as its trademark, symbolizing the fact that it, too, provides "forbidden" knowledge to those who buy and use its products. Incidentally, the logo shows an apple that has had a bite taken from it, thus reinforcing the Biblical connotations and associating the use of *Apple* computers and products with Eve, the mother of humanity).

Brand names or logos that are made to reproduce, imitate, or simulate a referent (what they stand for) are particularly effective in enhancing product recognizability. Such forms are known technically as *icons*. The *Apple* computer logo is an example of a visual icon, because it portrays its referent (an "apple") visually. In the *Russell & Bromley* ad, incidentally, there is one salient visual iconic cue that suggests a plausible interpretation of its overall meaning —namely, the vulvic configuration made by both the woman's legs and the folds of her skirt. The vaginal "V-shape" can also be seen in the shapes made by her arms and by her legs— which are mirror image V's.

Iconicity is a common representational strategy in advertising, involving any one of the human senses. Commercially produced perfumes that are suggestive of natural scents are iconic in an olfactory way, because they have been manufactured to simulate natural scents. Onomatopoeic jingles —*Plop, plop, fizz, fizz...* (*Alka-Seltzer*), *Snap, crackle, pop* (*Rice Crispies*), etc.— are iconic in an auditory way, because they simulate the sounds made by the products they represent. The choice by the *Guy Laroche* company of the name *Drakkar noir* for one of its cologne products, along with the pitch-dark appearance of the cologne bottle, entails acoustic and visual iconicity in a complementary way. The bottle has a ghastly, frightful black color, connoting fear, evil, the unknown. Forbidden things also take place under the cloak of the dark night; hence the name *noir* (French for "black"). The sepulchral name of the cologne, *Drakkar noir*, is transparently congruous with bottle design at a connotative level, reinforcing the idea that something dark, scary, but nevertheless desirous, might happen by splashing on the cologne. Indeed, the guttural *Drakkar* is manifestly suggestive of *Dracula*, the deadly vampire who mesmerized his sexual prey with a mere glance.

To reinforce product recognizability, some brand names and logos have been constructed *indexically*. An *index* is a sign that shows or indicates the relative location, direction, or orientation of something. The most typical manifestation of indexicality is the pointing index finger. Words such as *here, there, up, down,* etc., which refer to things in terms of their location, are also indexes. In the *Russell & Bromley* ad, the dark toes of the female's shoes point simultaneously to the product name and the "direction" of the path upon which the woman is seemingly about to take. Logos adopting arrow figures, such as those used by several courier companies, are typical examples of indexical trademarks.

Names and logos that have pure symbolic value are called, logically, *symbolic* signs. In semiotic theory, a *symbol* is a sign that has an arbitrary or conventional relation to its referent. Abstract words in general are symbolic signs. But any signifier —object, sound, figure, etc.— can be symbolic. A cross figure can stand for the concept "Christianity;" a "V-sign" made with the index and middle fingers can stand symbolically for the concept "peace;" and so on. The use of colors in advertising, for instance, is a symbolic representational strategy. The black and white contrasts in the *Russell & Bromley* ad —the white and dark tones of the shoes, the whiteness of woman's dress and purse, etc.— are symbolically connotative. In Western culture, *whiteness* connotes "cleanliness," "purity," "innocence;" *darkness*, in contrast, symbolizes "uncleanness," "impurity," "sensuality." So, in the ad, the white colors suggest the purity and sexual innocence of the female before she ventured through the portal, whereas the dark ones forebode an impending transgression of this state. And since the two are juxtaposed against each other, we can thus infer an erotic struggle within the female character. The detergent brand names *Sunlight* and *Ivory* are likewise evocative of connotations of "cleanliness" and "purity."

The preceding discussion can be summarized in chart form as follows:

Sign Type	Representational Technique	Examples of Product Names and/or Logos	Examples from the Russell and Bromley ad
icon	resemblance, imitation, or simulation	*Drakkar Noir* *Apple* logo	the V-shape of the hands, arms, and folds made by the dress
index	indication of location, direction, or orientation	logos made with arrows	the shoes pointing to the lettering and to the implied "underworld"
symbol	arbitrary relation to referents	*Sunlight* *Ivory*	the connotations of the white-dark contrasts

Product names and logos bear the meanings that they do, clearly, not in isolation, but rather, in relation to meanings already present in a culture. First and foremost, they must be differentiable from other products of the same kind. *Russell & Bromley* shoes must be perceivably distinct from other brands, qualitatively and connotatively. High heel shoes are high heel shoes, no matter what name they come with. But the differences in product quality and image are the things that make the *Russell & Bromley* shoes recognizably different from other pump brands. This differentiation relation is known technically as *paradigmatic* structure. It is the relation whereby some minimal feature (or features) associated with a product is sufficient to keep it differentiated from all other products of the same kind. Paradigmatic structure is a relation of *contrast*. It is found in all human meaning systems. For instance, early rock 'n' roll, as exemplified by, say, the first songs of Elvis Presley, is perceivably distinct as a musical form from the music of 1990s rap musicians; Italian words are perceivably distinct from English words (e.g. Italian words end typically in vowels, English ones do not); and so on.

Paradigmatic contrast also occurs at minute levels of signification. In the *Russell & Bromley* ad, the contrast between black and white tones entails a difference in connotative meaning — "innocence" vs. "maturity," "spirituality" vs. "sensuality," etc. This type of minimal contrast is found in all systems of human signification: e.g. in language, it can be seen in the binary contrasts among sounds (known as *phonemes*) that make it possible to keep words distinct (*pin* vs. *bin*); in music, it can be heard in the half-tone difference that sets major chords apart from minor chords; and so on.

In addition to contrast, signs bear meaning through the ways in which they combine with other signs or elements. Shoes are part of an overall dress code, *blending in* with other elements of dress. In the *Russell & Bromley* ad, the two-tone color of the pumps (black and white) blends in with the whiteness of the female's dress, the blackness of her hair, etc. The matching combination of colors in the ad is known as *syntagmatic* structure. This too is found in all human systems. In music, for instance, a melody is recognizable as such only if the notes follow each other in a certain way (e.g. according to the rules of classical harmony); in language, *pin* and *bin* show syntagmatic structure because the combination of sounds with which they are made is consistent with English syllable structure; on the other hand, *tpin* and *tbin* would not be legitimate words in English because they violate its syllable structure; and so on.

Paradigmatic and syntagmatic relations guarantee that signs have a discernible (repeatable and predictable) shape or form and that they "fit" together in patterned ways. Signs are like pieces of a jigsaw puzzle. These have visual features (signifiers) on their "faces" that keep them distinct from each other, as well as differently-shaped "edges" that makes it possible to join them together in specific ways to complete the overall jigsaw picture.

Textuality

The "jigsaw picture" that results from putting signifiers together is known, technically, as a *text*. The basic characteristic of texts is, in fact, that they deliver meaning by the ways in which their signifiers have been assembled. The *Russell & Bromley* ad, for example, is a text made with visual signifiers (pictures, colors, shades, etc.) that generate the signifieds mentioned above ("sexuality," "innocence," etc.), because they both contrast and blend in with each other in suggestive ways. The overall meaning of the text is not, however, the simple sum of the signifieds suggested by the signifiers (= paradigmatic structure); its meaning is derivable from the ways in which these have been put together (= syntagmatic structure):

- the woman's skirt is made of lace—a fabric with an "innocent" texture — matching the lace fabric of the curtains covering the portal;
- the folds of her skirt suggest the outline shape of a female genitalia — a shape reinforced by the configuration of the woman's arms and legs;
- the "feel" implied by the leather shoes and handbag is of a fetishistic nature;
- the young woman's contemplative state of sexual readiness, as can be read in her facial expression and posture, and as reinforced by the configuration of her legs and by exposed knees, which invite the viewer to gaze upon her sexuality, is an obvious voyeuristic "turn-on," as the saying goes;
- the woman's flowing, unrestrained hair suggests a willingness to experience sexual satisfaction (to "let go," as the expression goes).

Note that these elements cohere into a system of meaning that leads, as we hypothesized in the previous chapter, to a *narrative* interpretation of the text based on the mythical story of Persephone, the character who was abducted and raped by Pluto, the god of the underworld. Is the *Russell & Bromley* ad text truly a modern representation of this ancient mythic text? The answer would seem to be *yes*. A descent into the "underworld of sex" is suggested, for instance, by the fact that the woman is sitting on the top step of a staircase that is "leading downward." The steps of the staircase are made of concrete and are "cracked," the suggestion being that the underworld is opening up to engulf the woman. Symbolically, the portal leads from one state (innocence) to another (sexual maturity). The woman has just crossed its threshold, ready to be engulfed by the passions of the new realm. The lace-covered doorway and her lace dress are residues of her previous state. The woman is apparently suspended between the two states, as is the viewer. The tension that this creates is like the tension produced by sexual excitement. Will wearing *Russell & Bromley* shoes lead a young "girl" onto the path of sexual maturity?

Incidentally, the tactile feeling associated with a visual image (e.g. the lace dress, the leather shoes, etc.) is known as *synesthesia*. This is defined as an experience in which the stimulation of one sense elicits a perception that ordinarily would be elicited had another sense been stimulated, as when a loud noise registers as a blinding light, or vice versa. In our case, it is a visual image that evokes a tactile response. In all synesthetic experiences, the imagination takes over the functions of perception. The overall effect of mixing sensory modalities is called *aesthesia*, defined as a total sensory and affective response to a text.

The *textuality* generated by ads and commercials —i.e. the specific mode or modes of making them with certain underlying themes and with recurrent signifieds— is an intrinsic feature of the signification systems created for products. Thus, in addition to naming a product in order to evoke certain connotations, its image can be further entrenched by establishing a specific kind of *textuality* for it, i.e. by creating ads and commercials that are deliver recurrent themes, techniques, characters, styles, etc. to the consumer. The textuality associated with products can also be reinforced by jingles. The *Plop, plop, fizz, fizz, oh what a relief it is!* jingle for *Alka-Seltzer*, the *Snap, Crackle*, and *Pop* jingle for *Rice Crispies* are just two examples of how jingles and products can become intertwined textually. These typically impart a friendly, often humorous, quality to the product's image. Classical music can likewise be enlisted to convey a sense of superiority and high-class qualities to a product. Sometimes, it even becomes an integral component of the product's textuality. For instance, in the Ontario-based milk advertising campaign, *Drink milk, love life!* of the late 1990s (in which two of the authors of this manual were involved), the use of the *Ode to Joy* section of the fourth movement of Ludwig van Beethoven's (1770-1827) ninth symphony was added as an integral component of the product's textuality to impart a sense of joy to the drinking of milk by emphasizing the uplifting qualities of milk through the uplifting feeling evoked by the music. Textuality can also be established by creating characters on purpose to enhance product recognizability —e.g. *Speedy (Alka-Seltzer)*, *Ronald McDonald (McDonald's)*, *Tony the Tiger (Esso)*, etc.— or by having the product endorsed by famous personages — actors, sports figures, etc.

As Leiss, Kline and Jhally (1990: 5) have argued, at a most general level, textuality can be divided into *rational* and *non-rational*—the former is designed to appeal to the reasoning mind, the latter to the emotional mind. Rational textuality characterized advertising in the period from 1890 to the early 1920s. The print ads of that era focused on the utilitarian aspects of the product itself — its qualities, its price, its functions, etc. Non-rational textuality has characterized advertising ever since the 1920s. During the 1920s, 1930s, 1940s, and part of the 1950s print ads and radio commercials emphasized the symbolic attributes associated with a product —status, family, etc.; during the 1950s, 1960s, and part of the 1970s print ads and radio and TV commercials focused on creating an image for the product— glamour, romance, sensuality, etc.; since the 1970s, ads and commercials have emphasized image even more so.

The many manifestations of a product's textuality —through specific ads and commercials— is a primary contributor to establishing a system of signification for it. This ensures that the connotative signifieds associated with a product are given a certain stability. What can change in future representations of the product are the signifiers that deliver the same signifieds. Thus, for example, the *Russell & Bromley* ad, which goes back a number of years, could be updated by changing signifiers such as the hairstyle of the female, the type of clothes she wears, her bodily posture, etc. The new signifiers could then be organized to represent a more contemporary "view" of female sexuality and attractiveness in contemporary versions of the ad. The underlying mythic story could also be changed to reflect some other narrative portrayal of feminine sexuality (e.g. the myth of Diana, of Venus, etc.). But the signification system would remain the same. Returning to Barthes' idea of neomania (chapter 1), it can be said that the craving for new things is generated not only by changing some stylistic detail of the product (e.g. higher or lower heels, shape, etc.), but also by constantly updating the signifiers (visible images) that deliver the product's textuality. This is also a basic strategy for maintaining consumer loyalty. People seem to like the same things, with their constant meanings, but they also want to make sure that they are "in style," or "up to date," in what they buy.

Textuality is achieved by *encoding* connotations into ads and commercials, i.e. by using various codes to construct texts. The primary objective of semiotics in advertising is to unravel what codes have been used and how they deliver the meanings that they do — hence the term *decoding* to describe what the semiotician does. Encoding is, in effect, representation, while decoding is interpretation. Representation is a deliberate use of codes to capture, portray, simulate, or relay impressions, sensations, perceptions, or ideas that are deemed to be communicable and culturally meaningful. Interpretation is determining how texts make meaning. Assigning a name to a product, with all the connotations that this entails, involves the use of the *naming code* of a culture; the creation of logos or trademarks involves the use of the *symbolic codes* of a culture; the composition of jingles to impart a recognizable musical identity to the product involves, needless to say, a use of the *musical code* or *codes* of a culture, etc.:

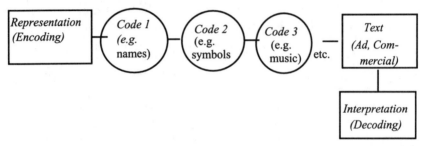

It is to be noted that both the maker of an ad or commercial and the interpreter must have access to the same codes. This simple model shows why semiotics is often called the science of decodification, for it aims to unravel the codes used in making up texts and the connotative meanings that these engender.

The Use of Multiple Media

The representational medium utilized to deliver the textuality associated with wearing *Russell & Bromley* shoes is *print*. There are, of course, other types of media that can be used in advertising to ensconce the same product's image—radio, TV, Internet, etc. In radio and television commercials, product textuality is delivered through an actual narrative format, and reinforced by linguistic and musical elements.

The print ad reaches people through *newspapers, magazines, direct mail*, and *outdoor signs*:

- Newspapers, on average, devote almost half of their space to advertising. These offer advertisers several advantages over other media. Most adults read a daily newspaper; and many specifically check the ads for information about products, services, or special sales. Newspaper advertising can also quickly incorporate a sudden demand for certain merchandise.

- Magazines have a number of advantages over newspapers. They are usually read in a leisurely manner and are often kept for weeks or months before being discarded. They also offer better printing and color reproduction.

- Direct mail advertising includes the use of leaflets, brochures, catalogues, and other printed advertisements that are delivered by a postal service.

- Outdoor signs are used because people pass by the signs repeatedly. In addition, large, colorful signs attract attention. The main kinds of outdoor signs include: posters, painted bulletins, illuminated displays, transit signs, window displays, and point-of-purchase displays.

Radio advertising has the advantage that people can listen to programs while doing other things, such as driving a car or working at home. Another advantage is that radio audiences, in general, are more highly selected by the type of programming than are television audiences. For example, stations that feature country music attract different kinds of listeners than do those that play rock. By selecting the station, advertisers can reach the people most likely to buy their products. Radio commercials include direct sales announcements, dramatized stories, and songs. Most commercials last 30 or 60 seconds.

Television advertising has become the most effective medium for delivering product image because it brings sight, sound, and action directly to consumers in their homes. Advertisers can explain and demonstrate their products to viewers who are enjoying a TV program and cannot easily avoid the commercials. Network television reaches a vast, nationwide audience at a very low cost per viewer. The majority of TV commercials consist of short spot announcements, most of which last 30 seconds to a minute. The commercials are usually run in groups of three to six. Television networks and stations generally limit commercial time to about 10 minutes per hour during prime time and 16 minutes per hour during most other broadcast times.

The Internet has become a highly effective medium of advertising since its advent in the 1990s. The Internet has made it possible for people all over the world to communicate effectively and inexpensively with each other. Unlike traditional broadcasting media, such as radio and television, the Internet is a decentralized system. Each connected individual can communicate with anyone else on the Internet, can publish ideas, and can sell products with a minimum overhead cost. Commercial use of the Internet is growing dramatically as more individuals gain access to it. Virtually any product or service can now be ordered from Internet sites.

Ad Campaigns

Another primary means of ensuring the delivery and social installation of product image is the *ad campaign*. This can be defined as the systematic creation of slightly different ads and commercials based on the same theme, characters, jingles, etc. An ad campaign is comparable to the *theme and variations* form of music—where there is one theme with many variations. Here are just a handful of examples of famous ad campaigns through the years:

- In 1892, the *Coca-Cola* logo appeared across the country, painted as a mural on walls, displayed on posters and soda fountains where the drink was served, imprinted on widely marketed, common household items (calendars, drinking glasses, etc.).

- In 1904, the *Campbell's Soup* company began its highly successful advertising campaign featuring the rosy-cheeked *Campbell Kids* and the slogan *M'm! M'm! Good!* The campaign is still ongoing as we write.

- In 1970, *McDonald's* launched its highly successful *You deserve a break today* advertising campaign that is still ongoing.

- In 1985, *Nike* signed basketball player Michael Jordan as a spokesman, marking the beginning of a dramatic growth for the company. *Nike* marketed the *Air Jordan* line of basketball shoes and clothes with a series of striking advertising creations (ads and commercials). Those creations, along with the company's *Just Do It* campaign featuring football and baseball star Bo Jackson and motion-picture director Spike Lee, boosted *Nike's* profits considerably. In 1997, *Nike* entered a new period of high-profile product image when company spokesman Tiger Woods became the first African American (and also the first Asian American) to win the Professional Golf Association's Masters golfing tournament.

- In 1991, the American Medical Association criticized *RJR Nabisco* for using a cartoon character named *Joe Camel* in its *Camel* advertising campaign, claiming that the campaign was targeted at children. In 1992, the US Surgeon General asked the company to withdraw its *Joe Camel* ads, and this request was followed by more government appeals in 1993 and 1994. The company responded to public concerns by promoting a campaign that encouraged store merchants and customers to obey the law prohibiting the sale of tobacco products to minors. In 1997, under increasing criticism, the company ended its *Joe Camel* ad campaign

- The growth of the *Gateway 2000* computer company in the 1990s was helped, in large part, by an unusual advertising campaign featuring employees standing in cow pastures. The company also shipped its computers in boxes splattered with black spots like those of Holstein cows, reflecting its Midwestern roots.

The most effective type of campaign is the one that adopts or coopts social themes. In the 1960s, for example, the image created by the media of self-proclaimed "rebels" and "revolutionaries," referred to generally as "hippies," who genuinely thought they were posing a radical challenge to the ideological values and lifestyle mores of the mainstream consumerist culture, ended up becoming the incognizant trendsetters of the very culture they deplored, providing it with features of lifestyle and discourse that advertisers have, since the 1960s, been able to adapt and recycle into society at large. Counterculture clothing fashion was thus quickly converted into mainstream fashion, counterculture music style into mainstream music style, counterculture symbolism and talk into society-wide symbolism and discourse — hence the crystallization of a social mindset whereby every individual, of every political and ideological persuasion, could feel that he/she was a symbolic participant in the "youth revolution."

The use of the hippie image in ads and commercials of the era occurred at a point in time when a dynamic business community decided it was in its best interest not to fight the images of youth insurgency, but rather to embrace them outright. One highly effective early strategy of this "if-you-can't-beat-them-join-them" approach was the development of an advertising style that mocked consumerism and advertising itself! The strategy worked beyond expectations. Being young and rebellious came to mean having a "cool look;" being anti-establishment and subversive came to mean wearing "hip clothes." The corporate leaders had cleverly "joined the revolution," so to speak, by deploying the slogans and media images of youthful rebellion to market their goods and services. "New" and "different" became the two key words of the new advertising and marketing lexicon, coaxing people into buying goods, not because they necessarily needed them, but simply because they were new, cool, hip. The underlying system of signification of this clever marketing strategy allowed consumers to believe that what they bought transformed them into ersatz revolutionaries without having to pay the social price of true nonconformity and dissent.

Campaigns, such as the *Pepsi Generation* and the *Coke* universal brotherhood ones, directly incorporated the images, rhetoric, and symbolism of the hippie counterculture, thus creating the illusion that the goals of the hippies and of the soft drink manufacturers were one and the same. Rebellion through purchasing became the subliminal thread woven into the pop culture mindset that the marketing strategists were starting to manipulate and control effectively. The *Dodge Rebellion* and *Oldsmobile Youngmobile* campaigns followed the soft drink ones, etching into the nomenclature of products themselves the powerful connotations of hippie rebellion and defiance. Even a sewing company, alas, came forward to urge people on to join its own type of surrogate revolution, hence its slogan *You don't let the establishment make your world; don't let it make your clothes.* In effect, by claiming to "join the revolution," advertising created the real revolution. This is why, since the late 1960s, the worlds of advertising, marketing, and entertainment have become totally intertwined with youth lifestyle movements, both responding and contributing to the rapid fluctuations in social trends and values that such movements entail.

Today, the advertising industry has appropriated "cool images" so completely that it is no longer recognized consciously as a form of lifestyle that emanated from a subversive movement of the young. Sociologically, the end result has been a further obliteration of the crucial emotional difference that traditional cultures have maintained between the social categories of *young* and *old*. This is why nowadays the rhetoric of youth is quickly transformed by advertising textuality into the rhetoric of all; why the fashion trends of the young are recycled and marketed shortly after their invention as the fashion styles of all; and why the fluctuating aesthetics of the youth culture are quickly incorporated into the aesthetics of society at large. Cultural cool has, in effect, become the social norm.

Practical Activities
(for Advertisers, Marketers, and media Students)

1. Identify and define the three main strategies used for enhancing product recognizability.
2. Give a common brand name and trademark (if one exists) for each of the following products/services, identifying the system of connotations it evokes and what kind of textuality is used for it.

Product/ Service	Brand Name /Logo	Connotations	Textuality
men's cologne			
women's perfume			
automobile			
insurance company			
cigarette			
dog food			
cat food			
detergent			
men's watch			
women's watch			
pain tablet			

3. Invent either an iconic, indexical, or symbolic brand name or logo for each type of new product/service.

Product/ Service	Iconic Brand Name/Logo	Indexical Brand Name/Logo	Symbolic Brand Name/Logo
cigarette			
courier			
eyeglasses			
furniture			
cereal			
automobile			
hotel			
bank			
travel service			
resort			
appliance			

4. Create systems of signification (brand names, logos, and textualities) for the following new product/service lines:

Product/ Service	Brand Name	Logo	Textuality
cigarette			
courier			
eyeglasses			
furniture			
men's pants			
women's pants			
family van			
beer			
wine			
pasta			
chocolate bar			

5. Suggest media or means other than those mentioned in this chapter for establishing product recognizability and image.

6. Describe ad campaigns you would design for the following new products:

a new automobile
a new computer
a new soft drink
a new cosmetic

3. Textuality

As mentioned in the previous chapter, *textuality* is one of the primary strategies used to enhance product image and recognizability. It inheres in creating a series of ads and/or commercials that deliver the same signifieds (meanings or themes), using similar kinds of techniques (e.g. characters, jingles, etc.). Product textuality works at two levels —a *surface* and an *underlying* one. The *surface level* constitutes the depiction or representation itself— and style in which ads and commercials have been created. The *State Farm* ads and commercials, for instance, invariably involve situations of family-based need which are met by the company through the intervention of friendly and neighborly agents who are always *there* (as the company's jingle puts it) in difficult times. The different ads and commercials are, in effect, surface variations of an *underlying* signification system structured around such meanings as "security," "safety," "family values," "friendliness," "trustworthiness," etc.:

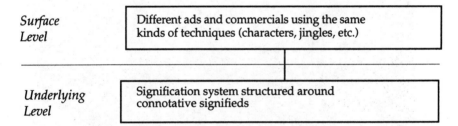

Surface Level — Different ads and commercials using the same kinds of techniques (characters, jingles, etc.)

Underlying Level — Signification system structured around connotative signifieds

Given its importance in advertising and marketing, the topic of textuality will be given separate treatment in this chapter. We will start off by decoding a typical print ad in order to illustrate concretely how surface and underlying levels correlate in the generation of textuality. Then, we will discuss the nature of underlying signification systems. Finally, we will describe some basic techniques, verbal and nonverbal, that are used in the construction of textuality.

Generating Textuality

Consider the following ad for a man's cologne named *Versus*, by *Versace*, which was taken from a lifestyle magazines several years ago.

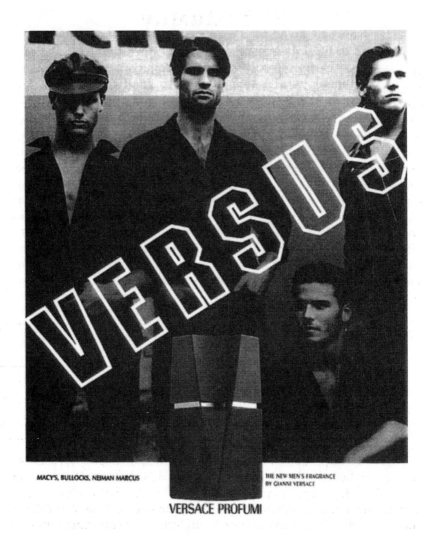

At first look, the ad seems simply to spotlight four rugged, handsome young men who presumably wear *Versus* to smell as good as they look. At this surface level, the ad seems to be merely saying: "To look as *cool* as these men, all you have to do is splash on *Versus*." But a more penetrating analysis will reveal that the ad is imbued with many subtle, symbolic innuendoes and allusions that transform it into a highly suggestive text.

To start off, consider the ad's most conspicuous iconic cues. The name of the cologne starts with the letter "V," the bottle displays a V-shaped intaglio in its shape, and the men in the ad wear either a shirt or jacket whose open collar makes a V-shape outline. At one level, this perfusion of V's strengthens the syntagmatic association between the cologne's name, *Versus*, and its manufacturer, *Versace*. But *Versus* is also a word that connotes "opposition" and "violation," and the V-shape is a symbol that connotes "indentation," "cleft," "fissure." This chain of connotations is reinforced by the fact that the word *Versus* crosses the entire ad, as if it were a line of separation between the men in the ad and the viewers of the ad.

So, what does the ad mean? Let's attempt a guess or, more appropriately, a few guesses. The ad is clearly aimed at affluent, young males who can afford to buy an expensive bottle of cologne. The men are, presumably, prototypes of what young urban professional males aspired to look like during leisure hours several years ago (when the ad was designed) — hours devoted to mate selection and/or sexual fulfillment generally. During the day, the men probably wear business suits; during recreational hours they wear "V-neck" apparel and dash on *Versus*. So, one possible interpretation of the ad's underlying meaning is that *Versus* can be used to aid men in their "sex-seeking" leisure activities. It is cologne designed to help them cross over, symbolically, from the work world to the leisure world —worlds that are in constant opposition. Now, reasoning mythically, one can argue that the former world is the realm of Apollo— the god of male beauty, the fine arts, and order —and the latter the realm of Dionysus— the god of wine, the irrational, and the orgiastic. Is *Versus* the olfactory means by which a modern Apollo can cross over into the erotically enticing Dionysian realm?

This mythic interpretation is strengthened by the fact that the V-shape of the men's collars and of the bottle design "point downwards," i.e. down towards the Dionysian underworld of carnality and sexual pleasure. The dark tones of the clothing and the bottle reinforce this mythic signified, suggesting that something dark and dangerous, but nevertheless desirous, is about to happen. *Versus* thus would seem to invite the male viewer to "cross over" into the dark underworld of sex where he can satisfy his "carnal nature." This world casts dark shadows on the men's faces —shadows that cover the eyes, the mirrors of the soul— for in the underworld, there is no soul, no spirituality, just carnality and ravenous cupidity. The V-shape intaglio of *Versus* hints at a crevice that is about to open up below a Dionysian world of lust and indulgence. Note as well that one of the men in the ad wears a leather hat and another a leather motorcycle jacket, both of which are synesthetically suggestive of sado-masochistic eroticism. To complete the interpretive picture being drawn, is the perfusion of V-shapes in the ad. The vaginal shape of the bottle, of the letter "V," and of the neck-line configurations are all suggestive of female sexuality.

But, there would seem to be at least one other interpretation of the text. One can ask, in fact, whether the object of the men's desire is not just the "opposite" of feminine sexuality, as the name *Versus* suggests connotatively. In other words, does the cologne allow the men to descend even further to satisfy deeply hidden homosexual desires? The good looks of the men, their darkened eyes looking directly into the camera, their muscular bodies and sensuously-protruding lips, the leather apparel they are wearing, and the conspicuous absence of women in the ad, are all strongly suggestive of this second interpretation.

At this point, we will bring our own analysis to a close. There are, in fact, other interpretations of the ad, as several subjects who viewed it upon our request emphasized to us (mainly students at the University of Toronto enrolled in a first-year semiotics class). Whether or not the two interpretations put forward here are legitimate is, actually, beside the point. The fact that both are possible, as are others, is what imparts a highly connotative textuality to the product. It is this textuality that can be used again and again in the creation of other ads and commercials for the same product.

Note that the two interpretations offered above were derived from establishing two *connotative chains* suggested by the ad's visual signifiers:

Connotative Chain 1

V-shape = femininity = sexuality = forbidden pleasures = sado-masochistic eroticism = etc.

Interpretation 1

Versus is a means to fulfill Dionysian sexual urges

Connotative Chain 2

darkness = leather = sexuality = forbidden pleasures = sado-masochism = hidden homosexual urges = etc.

Interpretation 2

Versus is a means to fulfill hidden homosexual urges

These chains constitute the underlying level of the product's textuality. The more chains there are, the more suggestive the product. In the same time period, other ads for *Versus* showed, in fact, similar surface presentations which appeared to deliver the same kinds of *connotative* meanings.

The Connotative Index

Whether or not the textuality conveyed by the *Versus* ads will induce consumers to buy the cologne is open to question. As mentioned in the opening chapter, it is certainly not the goal semiotics to determine this. The point of the above analysis was simply to illustrate that the key to unlocking the a product's textuality is to consider the surface signifiers of specific ads in a sequence, just like a comic strip, in order to see where the sequence leads in the underlying level. The Apollo/Dionysus *mythic text* suggested by the first connotative chain is known, technically, as a *subtext*.

Now, research conducted by the authors of the present manual on product image has suggested to us that the more interpretations there are —i.e. the more connotative chains ads and commercials generate in different subjects— the more likely is the product to appeal to subjects. This suggests a general principle of textuality:

Principle of Textuality

The higher the number of connotative chains generated by a product's textuality, the greater is the likelihood that it will appeal to consumers.

This relative number of chains —*high, average, low*— that a product's textuality tends to produce can be called its *connotative index*. Informal studies conducted by the authors of this manual several years ago have suggested that this is a valid notion. In one study, 10 subjects were given ads determined beforehand to have relatively *high, average*, and *low connotative indexes* through textual analyses such as the one conducted above. The subjects were asked simply to identify which of the ads they thought produced the most thoughts and meanings in their minds. There were 30 ads in all, 10 rated beforehand as having a *high index*, 10 as having an *average index*, and 10 as having a *low index*. The 10 with the *high index rating* (mainly perfume/cologne ads) were, in fact, identified by all 10 subjects as being highly suggestive and appealing. Some of these produced over 12 different interpretations (connotative chains). The subjects rated the remaining 20 ads as less suggestive, of which they considered 8 to be relatively more suggestive (= *average index*). These were ads for home products and services (insurance, detergents, etc.) that were also rated beforehand as having *average indexes*. The remaining 12 were identified as being the least suggestive by the subjects. Of these, only 2 were rated beforehand as having *average indexes*; the other were , in fact, also pre-rated as having *low indexes*. The latter were all taken from trade magazines announcing products and services in a straightforward "classified ad" manner, although pictures and various symbols were nevertheless used.

The above informal experiment was repeated several times with different subjects using different kinds of ads. Similar results were recorded each time. At the time of writing this manual, an extensive project at the Universities of Toronto and Lugano in this same area of research is producing results that are consistent with the previous findings.

Clearly, not all advertisements are designed to generate high connotative indexes. Classified ads, which are normally laid out simply to relay information about some product or service, have a 0 connotative index. The index is at a maximum in ads and commercials that promote the use of products associated with some aspect of lifestyle (perfumes, clothes, cigarettes, alcohol, automobiles, etc.) and at a minimum in classified ads. The index of every other type of ad or commercial falls somewhere in between these two extremes. The index can be conceived as a continuum, with 0 connotation (pure denotative or informational content) at one end and a maximum connotation point (open-ended, ambivalent, ambiguous content) at the other. Classified ads, ads in trade manuals, and the like tend to fall in the sector of the continuum nearest to the denotative end-point, whereas lifestyle ads tend to fall in the sector that becomes progressively more connotative:

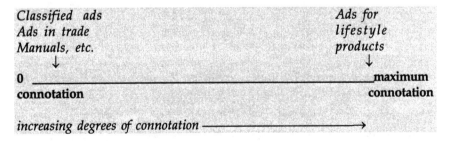

The idea of connotative index has been derived, in part, from Barthes' (1977) concept of *anchorage*, or the notion that visual images in some kinds of advertisements are polysemous (i.e. they have many meanings), which are *anchored* by consumers to specific socially-meaningful domains. Anchorage implies that ad texts with a high index are constructed in such a way that they can generate connotations from which the viewer can choose some and ignore others: i.e. the text's underlying connotative (associative) structure is anchored to specific meaning domains by different interpreters.

As mentioned above, the term *subtext* designates any text that the underlying level suggests through any of its connotative chains. A subtext is, in effect, a text implied or embedded within the main text. Indeed, an ad may suggest more than one subtext (as we saw above). More generally, the term *intertextuality* is used in semiotics to refer to the phenomenon that texts can be embedded into each other. Intertextuality is, in a phrase, the co-presence of other texts in a primary text. It should be noted, however, that the subtext could only be deciphered meaningfully (if at all) in specific cultural contexts. The connotations of darkness, oppositeness, etc. extracted from the *Versus* ad above would hardly be interpreted in Dionysian terms by people living in cultures where the Apollo/Dionysus myth does not exist. In other words, the interpretation of textuality will vary not only according to the analyst's whims, but also the specific culture in which the interpretation takes place. The components involved in the act of interpretation —the analyst, the text, the context, the code, the culture, the product, etc.— are inextricably intertwined.

As the analyses of the *Versus* and *Russell and Bromley* ads reveal, the subtext that can be extracted from the textuality of lifestyle products often has a basis in myth — the *Russell & Bromley* subtext alludes arguably to the myth of Persephone, and the *Versus* subtext to the myth of Apollo and Dionysus. Mythic subtexts are powerful because they act on the primordial parts of the psyche. And, indeed, the themes of the first myths have not disappeared from modern cultures; they continue to work at an unconscious level. As Roland Barthes (1957) cleverly demonstrated, in early Hollywood westerns, for instance, the mythic "good" vs. "evil" theme was symbolized by heroes wearing white and villains black hats. Sports events, too, are perceived symbolically as dramatic battles between "good" (the home team) and "evil" (the visiting team). The whole fanfare associated with preparing for the *World Series* of baseball or the *Superbowl* of American football, has a ritualistic quality to it that invokes the same kind of pomp and circumstance that ancient mythic armies engaged in before going out to battle and war. The symbolism of the home team's (= army) uniform, the valor and strength of star players (= the heroic warriors), and the strategic and tactical capacities of the coach (= the army general) stir the emotions of the fans (= the warring nation). The game (= the battle) is thus perceived to unfold in mythic terms.

Products themselves are intertwined with myth and ritual. Consider the *Russell & Bromley* pumps one more time. At a biological level, *shoes* have a very important function indeed — they enhance locomotion considerably. They are, at this denotative level, artificial locomotion-enhancing "extensions" of the human foot. But, as we saw, in social settings, shoes invariably take on a whole range of connotations. Up till the eighteenth century "shoe fashion" was the privilege of the aristocracy. The Industrial Revolution made possible the manufacture of fashionable clothes and footwear for the common person, making shoe fashion for the masses an economic possibility. Today, fashion trends and styles are dictated by media personalities, fashion moguls, and other high profile personages. Now, the broad range of social connotations associated with wearing high heel shoes cannot be eliminated from the product's modern-day textuality. To the outsider, the manifestations of sexual dressing may look arbitrary — after all, high heel shoes are rather uncomfortable (especially if the heel is high and thin). That's because sexual style is selective in a way that reveals itself. But to the individual living in a modern culture, they resonate as powerful symbols of sexuality.

Verbal Techniques

The surface text of both the *Russell & Bromley* and the *Versus* ads was a "silent" one, in the sense that the only meaningful words in them were the brand names themselves. Such texts nevertheless tell a story, as we have seen. But language is, more often than not, an important contributor to establishing the textuality of products. The use of verbal techniques to create effective advertisements and commercials —ads with attention-getting headlines, slogans designed to help create a favorable image of a company and its products, etc.— is a fundamental part of product textuality.

Consider the following ad for *Iron Cologne*, taken from a fashion magazine several years ago. At the surface level, the ad shows a handsome, muscular, sensuous man embracing a voluptuous woman. The shade of the ad text is bluish, the same color of the cologne bottle. At the bottom of the page is an insert showing the bottle of cologne being sprayed. The bottle is underneath the main visual text, as implied by the fact that the ad text itself has been "ripped" at its bottom right corner to expose the "hidden" cologne bottle. The expression *Pump some iron*, completes the text.

At a surface level, the message of the ad seems to be simply: "Enjoy a great sex life, as physically energetic and satisfying as *pumping iron*,

by wearing *Iron Cologne*." But delving a little deeper into its underlying layer of meaning reveals another story. First, the blue shading is not only in synch with the color of the cologne bottle, but it also suggests the "shadow of nighttime," an appropriate time period during which to carry out sexual activities. Note, further, that the male is pulling the female's hair forcibly. He is looking down at her. Her eyes, on the other hand, are shut submissively. We do not see where his other hand is (Could it be fondling her?). In short, the man is about to put the woman into a supine position for sexual intercourse. The implicit aggressiveness of the man's embrace is reinforced by the ripped insert at the bottom of the page. The act of ripping is forceful and passionate. And, finally, the exposure of the spraying bottle reveals what is really "underneath" the male's act of passion. His desire, in masturbatory terms, is indeed fulfilled in the form of a "spray" (= ejaculation?). Reinforcing this interpretation is the fact that the bottle is being sprayed in the same direction as the male's penile orientation. At a literal level the expression *Pump some iron* suggests that the strenuous activity associated with lifting weights will lead to a more robust romantic life. But at a metaphorical level it suggests something else that is more congruous with the ad's underlying meaning — *pumping* is indeed a metaphor for male masturbation and *iron* for the penis.

Figurative language, in fact, is a basic verbal technique used in generating product textuality. Consider two other ads as illustrative cases-in-point — one for the perfume *Volupté* and the other for *L'Effleur* fragrance products, both of which appeared in magazines several years ago. *Volupté* is designed to appeal to women in their twenties and thirties.

The first thing to note is that the perfume's name means "voluptuousness" in French. Second, the phrase *Trust your senses*, placed just below the perfume bottle, implies, at a literal level, that the buyer will be able smell the high quality of the perfume. But, then, the shape of the perfume bottle leads the buyer, subtextually, to infer a different story in the phrase. The dark, round bottle cap is highly suggestive of an aroused nipple —a sign of successful sexual foreplay. The phrase *Trust your senses* is suggestive of sexual "sensing," since a breast involves most of the senses in foreplay— sight, smell, taste, and touch. The background scene in the ad reinforces this interpretation, since it shows a secluded, dark place where the bottle (= female breast?) can be looked at voyeuristically through the beam of light that falls upon it.

In contrast, the *L'Effleur* ad spotlights flowers in the shape of a heart, emphasizing pure romantic love:

This theme of romance and sweet infatuation is reinforced by the woman's white dress, by the hug given to her by the little girl (a sign of innocent affection), and by the butterflies and angels embedded in the floral arrangement. In a phrase, the ad draws a picture of love as idyllic, bucolic, sentimental — a picture reinforced metaphorically by the little love poem about *First Love: Befitting and fragrant, we send bouquets, to the one who gave us yesterdays.*

As the analysis of these ads shows, the verbal part of textuality is also highly effective in delivering textuality. In addition to metaphor, there are a host of verbal techniques that advertisers use effectively. Some of these are as follows:

- *Jingles and Slogans*: These have the effect of reinforcing the recognizability of a brand name, since they tend quickly to make their way into communal memory: *Have a great day, at McDonald's, Join the Pepsi Generation;* etc.

- *Use of the Imperative Form*: This creates the effect of advice coming from an unseen authoritative source: *Pump some iron, Trust your senses;* etc.

- *Formulas.* Formulas create the effect of making meaningless statements sound truthful: *Triumph has a bra for the way you are; A Volkswagen is a Volkswagen;* etc.

- *Alliteration.* The alliteration, or repetition, of sounds increases the likelihood that a brand name will be remembered: *The Superfree sensation* (alliteration of *s*); *Guinness is good for you;* (alliteration of *g*), etc.;

- *Absence of language.* Some ads strategically avoid the use of any language whatsoever, suggesting, by implication, that the product speaks for itself.

- *Intentional omission.* This technique is based on the fact that secrets grab our attention: *Don't tell your friends about...; Do you know what she's wearing?;* etc.

In television and radio commercials the tone of voice, the sentence structure, and the use of various verbal ploys (jingles, slogans, etc.) are used to enhance product image. The tone of voice can be seductive, friendly, cheery, insistent, foreboding, etc. as required by product textuality. The sentence structure of ads and commercials is usually informal and colloquial, unless the ad is about some "high-class" product (e.g. a *BMW* automobile, a *Parker* pen, etc.), in which case it is normally more elegant and refined. In general, the type of sentence style used in ads and commercials is, as we have seen, a short imperative phrase—*Pump some iron, Trust your senses* —or aphoristic statement— *Somewhere inside, romance blossoms.* Advertising also borrows discourse styles to suit its purposes: a commercial can take the form of an interview; a testimonial on the part of a celebrity; an official format (*Name:* Mary; *Age:* 15; *Problem:* acne), and so on.

Nonverbal Techniques

The discussion of the surface presentation of the *Russell & Bromley, Versus, Iron, Volupté,* and *L'Effleur* ads focused primarily on visual signifiers. As the first three clearly show, facial expression in particular is extremely important as a visual signifier. The expression on the female in the *Russell & Bromley* ad, or of the males in the *Versus* ad, helped unlock the underlying meaning of the texts. In the *Iron Cologne* ad the male's expression conveys domination, control; the female's submissive sensuality. The face is a primary source of emotional communication. The lack of eye contact in the above ads also conveys a message. Looking in the eyes is a sign of love and affection. Looking away and closing one's eyes is a sign of sexual rapture and reverie. Visual images in advertising are absolutely critical in reinforcing product textuality. People can picture faces and images much more accurately and quickly than they can recall words. This is also why cartoon characters, computer graphics, and the like are used to endorse or represent their products. Mouthwash bottles dance across the screen; automobiles turn into animals; etc.

Another salient aspect of the *Russell & Bromley, Versus,* and *Iron Cologne* ads is the *bodily* forms of the personages — the females have a soft, slim body look, and the males a muscular and slim one. Body image —slim vs. fat, tall vs. short, etc.— is a powerful source of nonverbal signification. The association of slim with attractiveness, for instance, is formed in large part from media representations (in movies, ads, television, etc.). In our culture we tend to perceive corpulence negatively. But in all cultures, body size is not just a matter of physique, but also an issue of aesthetics. In contemporary Western society, the slim, lean look is a prerequisite for attractiveness for both males and females. The margin of flexibility from any idealized thinness model is larger for males than it is for females; but males must additionally strive to develop a muscular look.

Practical Activities
(for Advertisers, Marketers, and Media Students)

1. Collect several print ads of lifestyle products. Then fill in the following chart for each one:

Print Ad	Surface Level Nonverbal Signifiers Signifiers	Verbal	Textuality

2. Design ads for any lifestyle product based on the following connotative chains: i.e. for each chain construct an ad that renders it at a surface level—(1) identify the product; (2) give it a brand name; (3) design an ad for it:

a)*white = beauty = illumination = innocence = cleanliness = etc.*
b)*red = passion = sexuality = heat = etc.*
c)*smile = friendliness = trust = neighborliness = etc.*
d)*twilight = suspension of belief = eerieness = occultism = etc.*

3. Indicate which of the following products/services will, probably, have a low, mid, or high connotative index in its textuality:

Product/ Service	High Index	Average Index	Low Index
cigarette			
courier			
eyeglasses			
furniture			
men's pants			
women's pants			
family van			
beer			
wine			
pasta			
chocolate bar			
insurance			
real estate			
classified ad			

4. Invent slogans (jingles without music) for the following products according to the suggested verbal techniques:

Product/ Service	Metaphor	Alliteration	Formula	Imperative Verb Form
cigarette				
courier				
eyeglasses				
furniture				
men's pants				
women's pants				
family van				
beer				
wine				
pasta				
chocolate bar				
insurance				
real estate				
hotel				
bank				
travel service				
resort				
appliance				

5. Create textualities for the following products:

Product/ Service	Connotative Chain	Subtext
cigarette		
perfume		
cologne		
automobile		
men's shoes		
women's shoes		
family van		
beer		
wine		
pasta		
chocolate bar		
insurance		
real estate		

4. Semiotically-Based Research

Modern marketing is the business of getting products and services from producers to consumers in the most effective way possible. The main activity of marketing science today involves ascertaining ways in which product image for a specific group of buyers can best be enhanced. A basic marketing research technique is the survey of test markets to determine the potential acceptance of products or services before they are advertised. Through a process of careful questioning and investigation it is possible for an advertiser to learn what a consumer likes about an ad, a commercial, or an ad campaign. This process is, needless to say, fundamentally a semiotic one.

The present chapter discusses and illustrates the application of semiotics to market research. It starts, first, with a brief overall summary of the business of marketing. Then it describes in condensed summary form two case studies in which the authors of this manual were involved several years ago. Each one related to ascertaining product image through some aspect of brand naming. The actual names of the products and manufacturers are not provided. Finally, the chapter discusses several techniques that are hardly ever used in advertising and marketing research but which, in our view, hold great potential for the entire field. The work of the advertiser and marketer is, fundamentally, the work of the semiotician. Since consumers can choose from a huge variety of products and services, the process of ascertaining what signification system will make products and services attractive to customers has become a crucial one in today's marketplace. Marketers are involved, in effect, more in *selling signs* than in selling products (as the title of this book suggests).

Marketing Research

Market research is the scientific study of determining the probable users of a product or service. The results from the research lead to concrete suggestions for product development, including which products are to be manufactured. This allows manufacturers to meet the demands of the public by adding new products, changing existing ones, and dropping others. It also allows manufacturers to determine the best system of distribution of products and services and what the optimal pricing for these is.

Most business firms hire advertising agencies to create their advertisements and place them in the various media. In most cases, individual advertisements form part of an advertising *campaign*— an systematic method of advertising products and services that may run for several months, or more, and that usually involves more than one medium. The objective of the campaign may be to demonstrate a product's superiority over competing brands, to change the image of the product or company, or to achieve some other goal. The agency must also determine the target market—i.e. the people who are likely users of a product and at whom the advertising will be aimed. Finally, the agency has to estimate how much money and time will be needed to carry out the campaign. Information gathered from consumers provides the basis for determining the kinds of people at whom to aim advertisements, the types of signification systems to use, and in which media to place the ads. The chief kinds of market research include: (1) market research, (2) motivation research, and (3) media research.

Market research aims to determine the appropriate group on the basis of the age, sex, income, and occupation of potential consumers and their reactions to various brands. This type of information helps advertisers decide on the best way to present the features of their products. Motivation research attempts to find out why people buy certain products, through personal interviews, during which certain techniques developed by psychologists and sociologists are used. By discovering the motives for people's buying behavior, advertisers hope to find the most effective style of presentation to use in their advertisements. Media research involves measuring the size and makeup of radio and TV audiences at different times of the day, and of circulations of publications. Advertisers use information on audience size and makeup in selecting media in which to place ads. They then prepare a media plan that will give an effective combination of *reach* —the number of people who will see or hear the advertisement— and *frequency* — the number of times that they will see or hear it.

Case Study 1

The goal of marketing research is, essentially, unraveling what systems of signification fit best for a product or service and which media can optimally be employed to deliver the systems. In effect, marketing research is *applied semiotic research*. Two case studies in which the authors of this manual have been involved can be used to illustrate this very fact. The first case study involved a well-known baby food company, which had decided to introduce a new brand, X. The project aimed to ascertain the connotative potential that X had for typical mothers. To determine the signification system of X paradigmatically, a group of subjects was asked to compare X to two other well-known brand name baby food products —which we will call Y and Z— using the three words that best summed up their attitudes currently vis-à-vis commercially produced baby foods, and three words that would have best summed up their attitudes five years ago. These were subsequently discussed with the group. The subjects were then asked the following:

- What do you see as the strengths and weaknesses of the brands?
- What, if anything, does the brand offer that makes it unique?
- What one aspect of baby food or baby nutrition do you feel the brand excels in?
- What does each brand specialize in/focus on?
- What are your reactions on being exposed to the range of products within each brand, establishing whether or not the range is extensive enough and what additional products, if any, you would like to see?

In the case of the brand under study, X, the subjects were asked specifically: (1) what their reactions to it were; (2) what it stood for in their minds; and (3) what it brought to the overall line in terms of quality associations. Then, five "connotation-establishing" techniques were used: (1) a *collage* technique, by which the subjects were asked to cut out pictures from magazines that best represented the product, gluing them onto a surface; (2) an *imaginary world* technique, by which each subject was required to compare each brand to a world or land in terms of its topography, climate, architecture, society, values, lifestyle, attitudes towards child-rearing; (3) a *portrait chinois* technique, by which each subject was asked to identify each brand as a musical instrument, an animal, a film genre, a book, a weather system, a landscape, a gesture, an emotion, etc.; (4) a *picture association* technique, whereby each subject was required to picture a typical mother and baby who might use each brand, drawing and describing the home and the baby's room, and indicating how she pictured the manufacturers in this scenario; (5) a *slogan* technique, whereby each subject was asked to invent a slogan for each brand that best summed it up regardless of any slogans used in advertising for this purpose. The subjects were also asked to indicate what advertising, if any, they recalled having seen, read, or heard for any of the brands, and to comment on packaging, marketing initiatives, and expectations for each brand.

The reason for the above questions was, of course, to flesh out as many relevant connotations as possible associated with the products. After this, the group was asked to comment on a number of advertising concepts developed by the manufacturers, including:

- immediate reactions (first thoughts and feelings);
- understanding of the message (what impressions each one got from the brand);
- relevance of the message (Does it meet your needs or not?);
- uniqueness of the brand in relation to existing brands and adult food;
- attractive and unattractive aspects of the product;
- overall feeling (Does it strike you as personally meaningful and motivating or not?)

After revealing that these were all potential ways of communicating about X, they were asked which brand was:

- the most involving and motivating and why;
- the one that they would most want for their babies over all other alternatives;
- the one that fits best with what X could stand for in the future;
- how they would rank the brands X, Y, and Z.

The subjects were made up of 8 focus groups, 4 in each of New York City and Cleveland with participants recruited according to the brands they used and income level — lower income defined as annual household incomes of $30,000 or less; higher income as annual household incomes of $50,000 or more. The participants were all mothers of babies aged 3 to 24 months, who purchased baby food on a regular basis, serving jarred baby food at least five times a week. There was mix of working and non-working mothers and of mothers with one child versus more than one child in each group.

We will not go into the minute details that were collected here, nor will we break down the results quantitatively. Our purpose is simply to illustrate the kind of methodology that can be used to establish signification systems for products. Overall, it was found that the most relevant connotations to the mothers were the following two:

- Baby food should allow mothers to express a sense of love, warmth, comfort, and security through the feeding event.
- Like adult foods, it should offer the opportunity to introduce babies to the cuisine of one's culture.

In a market like Cleveland where its products are unchallenged, the manufacturer of X is seen as an established specialist offering quality baby food. Its image is based on a signification system related to home and warmth, generating feelings of trust and confidence. However, what some interpret as key strengths of the brand —tradition and security— others interpret as old-fashioned. Moreover, some mothers see the manufacturer as too concerned with nutrition at the expense of enjoyment. The same finding emerged in a market where Y is a serious competitor — X's advantage there too lies in generating a stronger image of warmth and love. However, Y's presence serves to emphasize even more X's outdated image, with the brand's perceived strength lying more in the past than in the future. Even among X users, there is a perception that X's packaging is far too old-fashioned, with the product descriptions used on the packaging tending to be overly bland. X is also at risk of being seen as insensitive to the current multicultural reality of the US. There is a need, in sum, for X to demonstrate an interest in becoming more contemporary.

X users in Cleveland admitted that, on a rational level, X and Z are both quality brands. However, on an emotional level they clearly felt more confident about X than Z. They associated X with trust, reputation, and longevity. Collages, which allow for the connotative chaining to occur spontaneously in iconic form, served to bring to the surface this major difference in signification systems:

X	Z
family	blandness
trust	lack of excitement
happiness	a pragmatic approach
comfort	reliability
growing up happy	growing up well
good eating habits	well-nourished

The imaginary worlds technique produced the following differences:

X	Z
rolling hills	flat, brown and dry landscape
trees, flowers and vegetables	concrete buildings, silos
fresh air	lots of noise
the smell of fresh-cut grass	robots
perfect climate	changeable weather
happy, cheerful atmosphere	lack of imagination
traditional, established	purposeful, focused
safe, carefree	achievement, accomplishment
wholesome values	following rules
relaxation, cycling, swimming	no leisure time
jazz	elevator music
harp, piano	trombone, drums
Alice in Wonderland	*Godzilla*
Leonardo di Caprio	Anthony Hopkins
Antonio Banderas	Jack Nicholson
reached by stork	reached by subway

Depictions of the X versus Z mother and child technique revealed the following differences:

X	Z
stay-at-home mother	career mother
outside life	inside life
holding child	child sitting separately
looking at child	child watching TV
focused on child	mother focused on something else
mother and child smiling	mother and child holding hands

As companies, X and Z were seen as very different, as reflected in the slogans devised for the two companies:

X	Z
Slogans focused on	
family business	big company
specializes in babies	baby food being just one division
knows the baby business	less knowledgeable
dedicated to children	profit-oriented
donating money to causes	profit-oriented
concerned with quality	profit-oriented
packaged with love	just packaged

Y and Z users in Cleveland (lower incomes) saw X and Z products as virtually interchangeable. The only distinction they made on the rational level is charted below:

X	Z
around a long time	offers less common products
nothing exotic	better value

Even the collages produced for both brands generated the same connotative chains: *emotional warmth = contentment = nutrition = freshness*. The imaginary worlds associated with each were, however, very different:

X	Z
large, safe	lots of texture
conventional	lots of color
uptight, structure, disciplined	happy
little communication	good interaction
reading, self-improvement	gardening, drawing
not experimental or adventurous	adventurous
piano	violin
predictable love story	drama
staid	willing to take chances
hunting dog	mutt

The X mother and child were depicted as living in an environment of contentment and calm, whereas the Z mother and child were depicted as living in an environment of stimulation and excitement. The two companies were also seen as very different:

X	Z
unchanging	youthful
stuck in a time warp	up with the times
knows the baby business	listening so that it can adapt to needs
dull	responsive

Higher income Caucasian Y and Z users in Cleveland saw more immediate differences between X, Y, and Z:

X	Y	Z
historical quality	pure fruits	newer on the market
experience	vegetables	less additives
well-known	visual appeal	home-made texture
good for older babies	expensive	economical

The collages produced the following connotative chains:

X	Y	Z
leader	appetite appeal	homey, comfort foods
research	naturalness	basic
information-sharing	purity	warmth

The imaginary worlds associated with each were:

X	Y	Z
NYC or Chicago	LA or Hawaii	farmland
high rise buildings	expensive	log cabins
technology	bright, vibrant	happy, content
advanced	colorful	unexciting
fast-paced, busy	creative	horseshoes
professional	artistic	casseroles
intelligent, efficient	experimental	family
computer games	children learning	money goes long way
Internet	opera, the arts	experience
balancing family and work	confident about child	nursing during lunch
organ	Hawaiian guitar	guitar
stability	adventure	comfort
dolphin	panther	dog

The mother and child relation was characterized as follows:

X	Y	Z
Gucci diaper bag	skinny, bare	child with cows, hay
professional	child with spiked hair	heavy-set
serious, no fun	colored hair	aroma of home-made
smart	child on skateboard	casserole maker

The companies were seen as:

X	Y	Z
technological	innovative	homey
pediatricians	baby-sitters	mothers

X users in New York City saw X, Y, and Z generally as follows:

X	Y	Z
variety	less variety	no experience
most popular	not around as long	too many additives
personal	right behind X	too rich

The collage exercise for X and Y produced few differences. Even the imaginary world exercise failed to produce distinguishable connotative chains between the two brands among the lower income Hispanic/African Americans in New York City who are X users. Both imaginary worlds were seen as:

- happy and healthy
- full of parks and playgrounds
- no crime and no violence
- innocent
- PBS, educational TV
- not polluted
- pure
- places in which all babies grow up to be lawyers or doctors
- without drugs
- emphasizing values of peace, love, happiness, and good nutrition

The manufacturers of both X and Y were seen as:

- meeting mother's needs
- employing lots of mothers
- understanding babies
- humane
- family-oriented
- not just in business for the money

The upper income Caucasians using X in New York City saw more differences between X and Y when constructing imaginary worlds:

X	Y
old-fashioned, traditional	modern, colorful
Disneyland	suburbia
1950s	1990s
wood	Formica
very brand loyal	open-minded
conservative, rigid	cool
non-working	stylish
washes and irons for husband	shares household tasks with husband
child-rearing	working
suburban house with picket	condominium
fence and dog	high rise dwellers
station wagon driver	independent thinker and buyer

There is further evidence of a somewhat dated side to X's image among the subjects, highlighted in the slogans they invented:

X	Y
	Slogans emphasized
old-fashioned values	making baby food to grow
convenience	healthy babies

Users in New York City saw X and Y differently as follows:

X	Y
popular	less commercialized
old	a specialist in baby food
specialized baby food producer	generalist in baby products
much product variety	more conscious of natural ingredients

The imaginary worlds task brought out the following differences:

X	Y
a factory or a Wall Street office	farms, green pastures
full of babies and insurance agents	cows, chickens, horses
very busy, noisy	clean, fresh air
focus on business, making money	focus on family
a marketing orientation	a product orientation
reached by company jet	reached by horse-drawn cart
Flintstones	*Wizard of Oz*
rock and roll	classical
drums	violin
intense	mellow
tiger	lamb

The X mother was typically depicted as pushing her baby in a stroller to buy toys, whereas the Y mother was portrayed as feeding her baby or going to the supermarket to buy food. The subjects saw the companies as:

X	Y
growth-oriented conglomerate	run by someone who knows babies
run by Mr. Big from an office	possibly run by a woman
on the top floor of a tower	focusing on quality
aloof	using baby food themselves
white, non-multicultural	employing all nationalities

Higher income Caucasian Y users in New York City saw the three brands as follows:

X	Y	Z
original	healthy	ketchup
around a long time	wholesome	pickles
basic, starter	wide selection	cheap

Their collage for X indicated a perception of the product as connoting age and tradition; the one for Y as connoting colorfulness, difference, and innovation; and the one for Z as only peripherally related to baby food. The imaginary worlds technique produced the following connotative chains:

X	Z
old buildings	casual
suits	jeans and T-shirts
history and old people	barefoot
honesty, the work ethic	heavy rock
rocking chairs on porches	one room schoolhouse
polyester	more emphasis on gymnastics
traditional schools	public education
uniforms	chaos
pencils	pleasant, well-meaning teachers
strict	frazzled

By contrast, the Y world was depicted as consisting of:

- mountains and beaches
- colorful, fun-filled
- containing lots of fruits and vegetables
- carefree, relaxed
- modern and up-to-date
- fitness and health-consciousness
- cotton
- Montessori schools
- laptop computers
- phonics and traditional math learning
- young, pretty teachers

The characterizations of the mothers were as follows:

X	Y	Z
prim and proper	yuppie	frumpy
Upper East Side	West Village	Mid West or Queens
kids in suits, perfect	Gap kids	holding onto child
drives a Volvo	sport utility	station wagon
husband is an accountant	producer	factory or construction worker

The three companies were seen as follows:

X	Y	Z
basic	young	unfocussed
reliable	up-to-date	wide interests
safe	new trends	trusted

With regard to packaging, there was a sense expressed even on the part of X users that the X packaging is old-fashioned, boring, outdated, and stodgy. Part of the problem, they suggested, was the lack of excitement in product descriptions used. Overall, it was felt that X should update its image through its packaging.

With regard to the concepts, all mothers felt that baby food manufacturers should ensure that their products: (1) help babies develop healthy eating habits by providing natural-tasting food, and (2) contain essential nutrients.

The perception of X as a brand associated with warmth, bonding, and the family is the signification system that best suits it. It was also felt that X continue emphasizing this system, not trying to expand its image to include the connotative chains generated by Y and Z. Overall, it would seem that for most mothers, X's traditional signification has a high connotative index. The only area of change would seem to be in packaging, which was seen unanimously as in need of updating.

Case Study 2

The second case study was commissioned by a company that operates a number of co-branded restaurant chains. The restaurant chains are labeled X, Y, and Z. A need was identified within the company to establish what is communicated to consumers by using combinations of brand names (X + Y, X + Z, Y + Z), in order to develop a long-term strategy for the company's portfolio. The overall objective of the study, therefore, was to establish the signification system generated at co-branded sites. The specific questions guiding the research issues were:

- Does co-branding dilute the signification system of individual brands or cause confusion?
- Are there real branding benefits or only operational benefits?
- What are the ingredients for successful co-branding?
- Can the individual signification system of each brand be maintained within the context of co-branding?
- Are there service performance requirements for each brand, and can staff distinguish between these and deliver different service patterns?

An evaluation of each combination of brands was conducted by an integration of semiotic analysis with anthropological ethnographic research. A semiotic analysis was undertaken beforehand of printed materials (menus, print ads, on-premises materials, internal documents and consumer communications), the physical appearance of outlets (design, layout, seating, spacing, decor). The analysis was complemented by ethnographic research involving systematic observation at three co-branded sites:

- X at X Plus (= proposed new branding) using the new decor and logos
- Y at X Plus, using the older 1997 decor and logos
- Y with Z

Advance notice was given to the manager at each site and the researcher introduced himself upon arriving. The researcher sat down at a table affording a full view of the premises and the service counter. While observation sessions lasted approximately six hours, lunchtime (11:30 to 14:30) was the period of reference for all three locations. A 15 to 20 minute discussion was also carried out with the manager at each site at some point during the observation period. Stops were also made at four other Y sites located en route to the three main sites to gather comparative data.

Co-branding need not dilute the signification systems of individual brands or cause confusion, provided it is additive. For co-branding to be additive, the systems of each brand should ideally be integrated into the new designation with both retaining their whole connotative range. If this cannot be maintained, the "default" brand meaning should be the one that "takes over" the other. This means, for instance, that in an X restaurant serving Y products, the X meanings should be kept intact with the Y meanings added on, and vice versa.

There can be real branding benefits as well as operational ones with additive co-branding. The co-branding of *Chapters* with *Starbucks* illustrates this, with both sharing connotations of order and organization, with the intellectual connotations of *Chapters* being additive to the gourmet ones of *Starbucks*. This additive effect means that co-branding *Chapters* with *Starbucks* results in a "mind-body" signification system, focusing on the individual who enjoys the finer things in life, and is cultured in a well-rounded way.

The prerequisites for successful co-branding are therefore two brands with some connotations that are shared and others that are different but compatible and complementary. The individual meanings of each brand can be maintained within the context of co-branding. However, this implies that the signification systems of each must be constantly reinforced and that no changes be implemented that may undermine the value of the "default" brand.

It was found that the different service requirements of X and Y are compatible. Service at X requires attentiveness within the context of the ordering and dining experiences while service at Y requires attentiveness within the context of the ordering and preparation experiences. Thus, X and Y appeared to be not only compatible but consistent with achieving additive co-branding through X Plus and Y Plus. The common sign linking the two was attentiveness, which can be delivered within both the X Plus and Y Plus contexts. It was found, however, that there were signification system differences with regard to Z, especially between Y and Z, resulting in a subtractive effect for Y.

While there is no evidence that the availability of Y products in X Plus outlets is subtractive, whether or not there would be additive value in promoting Y products more overtly is unclear. However, the effect may be additive, since Y shares values of cleanliness, safety and quality with X and may add a dimension of youthfulness and individualism to the new amalgamated signification system. The Y Plus co-branding experience turned out to be more clearly an example of additive co-branding. As executed, the core system of Y would be maintained with the availability of X products underscoring existing quality connotations and being an extension of the principle of freedom of choice. As in the case of X Plus, however, care must be taken to preserve all of the elements of the Y experience intact in the future.

The Y serving Z experience turned out, as mentioned, to be subtractive. Behavior observed in this co-branded environment suggests that there is inconsistency between the meanings of Y and Z. Y customers seemed to resolve this inconsistency by ignoring Z. However, the more successfully Z is promoted within the Y environment, the greater the risk that the signification system of Y will be changed from that of a superior fast-food outlet offering freedom of choice to that of an inferior fast-food outlet offering poor nutrition and standardization.

The follow-up research areas were then recommended:

- to conduct qualitative research using projective techniques to understand the current equity of Z and provide guidance in terms of how best to develop the brand, either within a stand-alone or co-branded context;

- to conduct quantitative exit interviews at key co-branded sites to measure customer reactions and brand perceptions to validate the hypotheses of this evaluation;

- to extend the semiotic and ethnographic evaluation to other co-branding contexts, both existing and potential.

Co-branding is, in a manner of speaking, a kind of "semiotic chemical mixture," whereby the connotative meanings of two signs fuse into a new one. For any co-branding mixture to be additive, it is imperative to ensure that the signification systems of each brand individually are maintained.

A semiotic analysis of the printed materials provided by the company suggested the following. First, X, which is intended to be a chain of casual family restaurants, generates the following connotative chain:

- a homey environment
- a relaxed, non-urban environment
- freedom from stress
- freedom from pretensions
- a change from home
- a change that is clean, safe and efficient
- different without being exotic
- tradition.

Its menu complements this chain, since it generates the following connotative signifieds:

- healthy, nutritious meals with rotisserie chicken emphasizing protein prepared in a relatively healthy manner;
- meals the whole family can enjoy, with chicken being almost universally acceptable and a safe choice.

Y, which is intended to be a chain of quick service restaurants, generates the following connotative signifieds instead:

- a chain where someone is responsible, conveyed through the use of a personal name (as in the case of *Wendy's* and *McDonald's*);
- homey, implied by the use of the genitive in its brand name;
- speed and efficiency through the use of a single word (rather than *Burger King* or X);
- but personalization too, through the use of a first name (as in the case of *Wendy's*, but not *McDonald's*);
- an informal and youthful appeal, based on a personal relationship on a first-name basis, rather than the all-family appeal of X.

Its menu complements this system, since it generates the following connotations:

- somewhere young people and people young at heart can enjoy the foods they like, the logo placing the emphasis on the food rather than the environment;
- an aspirational appeal to teens and young adults who want to distance themselves from the child orientation of McDonald's;
- a way for adults who are concerned about what they eat to feel good about foods they enjoy;
- good quality fast food, the method of preparation distinguishing Y from junk food;
- individuality and a recognition of the existence of personal preferences.

Z, which is intended to be a chain of fast food restaurants serving chicken, generates the following connotative signifieds instead:

- the speed and efficiency of a fast food outlet with its use of a single name;
- lacks the sense of someone being responsible (Z being an unusual surname with institutional overtones);
- lacks the personal touch of a first name;
- theoretically conveys trust, stability and positive values, although the association with fried chicken contradicts this.

Its menu complements this system, since it signifies:

- fast food, with the logo focusing on chicken as the source, without much redeeming value;
- unhealthy food / junk food;
- an indulgence for individuals who are not discriminating about quality and nutrition;
- lower socio-economic status and obesity because of the brash visual approach and overt connection with fried chicken.

In sum, from a semiotic perspective, it turned out that only concern for the company would co-branding Y and Z, which could be subtractive. For the co-branding to work, Y must remain the "default" brand —i.e. all the connotative meanings of Y must remain intact, with the Z meanings being added on. This also entails that all else remains intact — e.g. that Y service be provided.

Other Methods

The discussion in the previous chapter about connotative indexes suggest a method that, as far as we know, has probably never been used in market research. The method would be to simply ask subjects ask what a particular ad means. In line with the *Principle of Textuality*, the ability of respondents to figure out the subtextual features of ads would be inversely proportional to the ad's effectiveness: i.e. the more the respondents are aware of the ad's subtext, the less effective will it be as a persuasive text. The power of the text lies in its ambiguity and dense connotative layering. An ad whose signifieds can be easily figured out works mainly on a denotative level, and its overall effect is thus minimal.

The effectiveness of high connotative indexes is seen easily at Christmas time when gifts for children become highly charged with connotations. At no time in recent history have the effects of connotation been so conspicuous as during the 1983 Christmas shopping season. If the reader has forgotten, that was the period of the "Cabbage Patch" doll craze. Hordes of parents were prepared to pay almost anything to get one of those dolls for their daughters. Scalpers offered the suddenly and unexplainably "out-of-stock" dolls (a marketing ploy?) for hundreds of dollars through the classified ads. Grown adults fought each other in line-ups to get one of the few remaining dolls left in stock at some mall toy outlet.

How could a toy, a simple doll, have caused such mass hysteria? To a semiotician, only something with a high connotative index could have possibly triggered such intense commotion. The Cabbage Patch dolls came with "adoption papers." This was a concrete clue as to what the dolls really signified. Each doll was given a name —taken at random from 1938 state of Georgia birth records— which, like any act of naming, conferred upon it a human personality. And, thanks to computerized production, no two dolls were manufactured alike, as different from each other as two human beings. The doll became alive in the child's mind, providing the precious human contact that children living in nuclear families with both parents working desperately need. Dolls are "people substitutes." In some cultures, one is purported to be able to cause some physical or psychological effect on a person by doing something to a doll constructed to resemble that person. In our culture, children, and adults for that matter, "talk" to their dolls, who are felt to lend a receptive ear to their owners' needs and frustrations. Dolls answer a deep need for human contact. No wonder, then, that the Cabbage Patch episode was such an hysterical one. Parents did not buy a simple doll, they bought their child a sibling.

Perhaps the most effective technique that can be used by marketers to flesh out what an ad text means or connotes to people is the so-called *semantic differential*, invented in 1957 by C. E. Osgood, G. J. Suci, and P. H. Tannenbaum — a technique used widely by semioticians interested in advertising.[1]. The technique consists in posing a series of questions about a specific concept —*Is it good or bad? weak or strong?* etc.— as seven-point scales, with the opposing adjectives at each end. The answers are then analyzed statistically in order to sift out any general pattern from them. Consider a hypothetical example. Suppose that various subjects are asked to evaluate the concept *President* in terms of scales such as the following:

young	_	_	_	_	_	_	_	*old*
	1	2	3	4	5	6	7	
practical	_	_	_	_	_	_	_	*idealistic*
	1	2	3	4	5	6	7	
modern	_	_	_	_	_	_	_	*traditional*
	1	2	3	4	5	6	7	
attractive	_	_	_	_	_	_	_	*bland-look-ing*
	1	2	3	4	5	6	7	
friendly	_	_	_	_	_	_	_	*stern*
	1	2	3	4	5	6	7	

An informant who feels that the *President* should be modern, would place a mark towards the *modern* end of the *modern-traditional* scale. One who feels that a *President* should not be too young or old, would place a mark near the middle of the *young-old* scale. An informant who feels that a *President* should be bland, would place a mark towards the *bland* end of the *attractive-bland* scale; and so on. If a large number of informants were asked to rate the term *President* in this way, then it would be possible to draw an ideal profile of the *presidency* in terms of the statistically-significant variations in connotation that the term evokes. Interestingly, research utilizing the semantic differential has shown that, while the meanings of most concepts are subject to personal interpretation and subjective feelings, the range of variation in interpretation is not random, but forms a socially-based pattern. In other

---

[1] *The Measurement of Meaning*. Urbana: University of Illinois Press, 1957.

words, the use of this technique has shown that connotation is constrained by culture: e.g. the word *noise* turns out to be a highly emotional concept for the Japanese, who rate it consistently at the ends of the scales presented to them; whereas it is a fairly neutral concept for Americans who place it in the mid range of the scales. This same technique can, clearly, be used to flesh out the meanings of any ad text presented to subjects: e.g. by using scales such as *sexy-unsexy, friendly-unfriendly, aggressive-unaggressive,* etc. one can flesh out the connotations that a text will elicit.

Practical Activities
(for Advertisers, Marketers, and Media Students)

1. Using Case 1 as background, flesh out the product image of an automobile of your choice with a group of students in the class. Use the following techniques:

Collage	Imaginary World	Portrait Chinois	Picture Association	Slogan

2. Now, identify the primary connotative chains generated by the automobile. What would your recommendation be to the manufacturer who wishes to change its image?

3. Using Case 2 as background, determine whether co-branding a popu-
    lar donut shop chain with a cineplex chain would be additive or
    subtractive. Use real brands.

Donut Chain's Signification System	Cineplex Chain's Signification System	New Signification System

4. Using the notion of connotative index, first carry out an analysis of
    a 10 ads for different lifestyle products (taken from different
    magazines). Then, ask a group of people (e.g. other students in the
    class) what each ad means to them. On that basis, assign a
    connotative index to each ad (high, mid, low):

Ad's Signification System Determined in advance	Subject's Decipherment	Connotative Index
1.		
2.		
3.		
4.		
5.		
6.		
7.		
8.		
9.		
10.		

5. Using the notion of semantic differential, set-up various scales to
    flesh out the connotations of well-known brands of the following
    products or services:

    automobile
    perfume
    insurance company
    toothpaste

5. Synthesis and Concluding Thoughts

It is no exaggeration to claim that advertising has become one of the most powerful forms of social discourse in history. Starting out as a simple "pitch" to make products and services better known in antiquity and the medieval periods, it has become a means of text-making that shapes values, aspirations, lifestyle. In a world where the marketplace dictates morality and ethics, it is little wonder that advertising and marketing run the social show, so to speak. It is ironic to contemplate that all this came about through the inadvertent efforts of those espousing Puritanical morality and ethics — the very antithesis of advertising epicureanism. The Industrial Revolution of the nineteenth century was fostered and controlled initially by people with Puritanical values, who associated the accumulation of goods with the gaining of spiritual favor. As a consequence, such values unwittingly legitimized the emerging discourse of advertising at the time. The advertiser at first complemented the messages proclaimed by preachers. But shortly thereafter, with the spread of industrialism and the need to generate profits through increased consumption, the advertiser came progressively to take over the role of the preacher. And, indeed, there is a sermon in each advertisement. In a sense, advertisers devote themselves to proclaiming the consumerist faith and the means of attaining paradise on earth through consumption. Ironically, advertising is now being attacked by both "right-wing" Puritanical groups for promoting secular humanism and sexual immorality and by "left-wing" ones for deceitfully influencing and promoting stereotypes and useless socially-damaging trends. But what both sides seem to have ignored is that advertising is really the messenger, like the preacher was; blaming the messenger for the message is unwarranted. Even right-wing and left-wing now resort to advertising for their various causes! And, when the social message will change, so will advertising.

As we have attempted to show in this manual, to the semiotician advertising is extremely interesting not because of its social implications, but because it manifests how signs are used in a specific domain of human meaning-making. The corollary to this interest has, of course, a practical implication — namely, that semiotics can be of great service to the study of advertising and marketing. The primary goal of this guide has, in fact, been to show how semiotic method can be used in this

81

domain both as a theoretical and a practical tool. In this final chapter, we will synthesize the main points made in previous chapters and then offer our own critical reflections on the advertising industry and on the effects of advertising.

The Advertising Industry

Advertising has become a vital cog in the global industrial machine. The United States has the largest advertising industry in the world, with its center in New York City, where many of the major agencies have their headquarters. There are about 6,000 advertising agencies in the US, ranging in size from one-person organizations to huge agencies with several thousand employees. An advertising agency's chief function is to create and place advertising for clients. Most large companies have an advertising department. In some, the department prepares all the company's advertising and so functions as an in-house agency. Among those firms that employ an advertising agency, the company's advertising department works closely with the agency. Some companies that manufacture a large number of products have even brand managers, who supervise the advertising and promotion of products. It is clear that, as we start the twenty-first century, advertising and business economics have become two sides of the same coin.

The advertising industry has now established associations that work to promote the industry and to raise the standards of advertising. The leading national advertising organizations include the *American Association of Advertising Agencies*, the *American Advertising Federation*, and the *Association of National Advertisers*. Two other important advertising organizations are the *Advertising Council* and the *National Advertising Review Board*. The former prepares public service ads, such as those that promote highway safety and energy conservation; the latter fosters self-regulation of the advertising industry, evaluating complaints about deceptive advertisements. If the council judges an advertisement to be false or misleading, it asks the advertiser to discontinue it. Most governments in industrialized countries, moreover, have laws designed to protect consumers from deceptive advertising. They also have regulations that prohibit certain kinds of advertising. For example, a federal law in the US currently bans cigarette advertising on radio and television. But the Supreme Court of the United States has ruled that advertising and the advertising industry have some protection under the First Amendment to the US Constitution. Thus, regulations concerning advertising must be no more restrictive than necessary to accomplish the goals of state and federal government.

Laws on advertising differ in other parts of the world. In Australia, for example, most ads must be produced locally. China charges higher rates for foreign advertisers than for local companies or joint ventures. Agencies throughout the world support the *International Advertising Association*, which has headquarters in New York City. This organization works for truth in advertising, the protection of commercial speech, and improvements in the quality of media research.

The majority of jobs in advertising require a college education or special training. Approximately 30 colleges and universities in the United States offer major programs in the field of advertising. People with education in the liberal arts, journalism, behavioral sciences, business, semiotics, or commercial art may also find employment in the advertising industry. Information about careers in advertising are obtainable from the *American Advertising Federation* in Washington, D.C., and from the *American Association of Advertising Agencies* in New York City.

Overview of Semiotic Method

The essence of semiotic method is identifying and understanding how signs are used to represent something. In the case of advertising that something is usually a need, a desire, etc. As a form of representation and social communication, advertising is a sign-based process, i.e. a process that entails signification. Knowing which signifiers to use to convey advertising messages is the essence of the trade of advertising. Advertising is all about *signification* through skillful *representation*. In line with the fundamental *Law of Marketing* alluded to in the opening chapter, it is a form of text-making that is geared towards enhancing the saleability of a product or service by associating it with some desire or need through some culturally-significant *representational* process. It is not important that one or the other *interpretation* of an ad is the correct one; what counts is that an interpretation is possible in the first place. In fact, the more interpretations there are, the more likely the effectiveness of the ad. The effectiveness of an ad, commercial, or ad campaign varies according to the suggestive ideas it generates; the more suggestive, the more effective, thus enhancing product saleability.

The underlying messages of advertising now permeate commercialist societies. These offer the hope of more money, better jobs, security against the hazards of old age and illness, popularity and personal prestige, praise from others, comfort, increased enjoyment, social advancement, improved appearance, better health, erotic stimulation, and many more. The trick is selecting the appropriate signifiers to portray the messages to a specific target audience.

Semiotics can help advertisers create and sustain an acceptable product *image*. An *image* is a particular kind of sign that generates a system of meaning, or *signification system* for a product. Images are established through the use of four main representational techniques: (1) the use of a brand name that embodies the signification system; (2) the use of a trademark or logo that communicates the same system; (3) the creation of a slogan and/or jingle that reiterates and reinforces the same system; (4) the production of ads and commercials delivering the system.

As we saw in the previous chapter, brand naming is a crucial element in product signification. The names given to products will evoke certain images or systems of *meaning* in a regular way. They do so by evoking connotations, rather than denotative meanings. Buying a *Mercedes* automobile entails buying prestige, attractiveness, etc. Buying a *Dodge van* entails, instead, buying family-based connotations. Connotation is built as well into logos, slogans, and the actual ads and commercials created to advertise products. As we saw, by means of techniques such as the semantic differential, collages, portrait chinois, imaginary world association, etc. it is a straightforward task to evoke the connotative system that subjects associate with certain brands. Unlocking the signification system delivered by ads —which is often represented in the form of a mythical subtext— is the key to establishing advertising effectiveness —the more connotative associations generated by ads and commercials generate in different subjects— the more likely is the product to appeal to subjects.

This relative number of associative chains —*high, average, low*— that a product's textuality tends to produce was called its *connotative index*. The case studies described in this manual have suggested that this notion can be used profitably by market researchers to flesh out the effectiveness of certain brand names, ad campaigns, forms of packaging, logos, and the like. Since not all advertisements are designed to generate connotative indexes, the index can be conceived as a continuum, with 0 connotation (pure denotative or informational content) at one end and a maximum connotation point (open-ended, ambivalent, ambiguous content) at the other.

The *textuality* generated by ads and commercials —i.e. the specific mode or modes of making them with certain underlying themes and with recurrent signifieds— is an intrinsic feature of the signification systems created for products. Thus, in addition to naming a product in order to evoke certain connotations, its image can be further entrenched by establishing a specific kind of textuality for it, i.e. by creating ads and commercials that are deliver recurrent themes, techniques, characters, styles, etc. to the consumer.

The Effects of Advertising

In this section, we will take the liberty of removing our hats as semioticians, and put on our hats as social critics. Our intention is certainly not to blame anyone, but simply to voice our concern as citizens of a culture where advertising has become an integral component of meaning-making. Certainly, advertising has been good for economics. Although some economists believe that a large amount of the money spent on advertising is wasted, arguing that much advertising simply leads consumers to switch from one brand of a product to another brand, thus having no positive effect on the overall economy, there is no doubt that, without it, we would be living in a vastly different economic universe, not to mention psychological one. For one thing, it is the fuel for the economic engine that runs the mass media and mass entertainment industries. Advertising pays all the costs of commercial television and radio, for instance, providing everyone with free entertainment and news programs, even though many people may be irritated by commercial interruptions. Advertising also pays three-fourths of the costs of newspapers and magazines. Without advertising, readers would have to pay a higher price for newspapers and magazines, and many of the publications would go out of business. Because the mass media depend on advertising to stay in business, some social critics question whether advertisers control the media. They maintain that dependence on advertising lowers the quality of TV programming. In order to sell advertising time at high prices, TV networks try to attract the largest possible audience. Critics argue that the stations therefore broadcast too many general entertainment programs and not enough informational and cultural programs.

Advertising has extended its reach into virtually all domains of social interaction. For example, advertisements are now seen in movie theaters and on videotapes and DVDs prior to the featured movie. Ads appear on ski lift towers, and in high school classroom news programming. In supermarkets, shoppers may be exposed to in-store radio, grocery carts with miniature billboards or video screens, and TV sets with programs or commercials in the checkout line. Realizing that the same kinds of persuasive techniques could be used to promote candidates, in 1952 even politics got into the "advertising game," when Dwight D.

Eisenhower successfully ran for the US presidency, with the help of advertising executives, who directed Eisenhower's presidential campaign. No wonder, then, that, since 1952, advertising has played an increasingly important role in political campaigns, with TV spot announcements having become a major strategy of campaigns for public offices at all levels of government. "It pays to advertise," has become the aphorism of the contemporary world.

Advertising is, in effect, a modern-day form of magic. The manufacturers of such products as gasolines and headache remedies, for instance, boast of new, secret ingredients — in the same way that magicians would use secret charms, spells, and rituals in seeking or pretending to cause or control events, or govern certain natural or supernatural forces. Like magic, advertising promises implicitly to produce marvelous effects through supernatural or occult powers. Advertisements may indirectly suggest that a mouthwash or a toothpaste will magically transform an unpopular person into a popular one. Consumers will buy these for the magic qualities suggested by such advertising, without critical thought. As we have seen throughout this text, advertisers use suggestion in many ways. No advertiser would dare guarantee that a person will become popular by using a certain product. But the advertisements may strongly suggest this result.

The greatest critique of advertising was leveled, as we have discussed previously in this manual, by the semiotician Roland Barthes, who claimed that it fostered a culture of neomania, a state of groupthink that artfully propels people to buy products they do not need or want. The spread of advertising throughout the cultural order since the 1950s has, as a consequence, been accompanied by criticism of this very effect it has had on cultural behavior. For example, as early as 1957, *The Hidden Persuaders*, a book by Vance Packard, became a best seller because it alerted the general public to the dangers of neomania. More recently, critics have accused advertising of generating a hedonistic and epicurean worldview. Lifestyle advertising in particular is seen as mirroring how contemporary humans in the mass perceive reality — as a collage of images that promote physical and social desires. The subtext of advertising is criticized for conveying the message that the only meaningful thing to life is enjoyment, prestige, security, attractiveness, etc. In the past, these would have been considered either sins or manifestations of vanity. Advertising is also trenchantly criticized for providing messages of assurance that consumption in itself can solve all human problems —perhaps even prolong life indefinitely and thus conquering death. Viewing the world through a television commercial or through magazine ads is bound, eventually, to transform the human view of the real world into a gaze that interprets it as if it were a TV program or a scene in an ad. Day in and day out advertising's fragmented images of life are bound to influence our overall view that reality is illusory and surreal— satisfying desires is the only thing that counts.

The language of advertising has also had an effect on the language of ordinary communication. Advertising language reduces thoughts to formulas, stock phrases, jingles, slogans. Its conceptual system is not tied to a larger social, religious, or philosophical grammar. It is instantaneous, geared to encapsulating fleeting images and condensed thoughts. Traditionally, the religious forms of discourse —gospels, catechisms, sacred books, etc.— have always had, as one of their intents, the promulgation of the "good news" about the origin, development, and destiny of humanity. This is, in fact, the meaning of the word *gospel*. Today, the good news is being announced by advertisers. Advertising now constitutes a form of discourse that celebrates consumption; it is the liturgy of consumerism. But this new catechism has no "divine author" with meaningful "answers to life." Its discourse categories merely announce that: "If you buy this or that, then you will be eternally young, sexy, happy, etc." No wonder, then, that mythic-religious themes pervade modern advertising. What is implicit in the advertising discourse is consumeristic prophecy — a postmodern replacement of eschatological prophecy which once proclaimed the immanence of the afterlife in the present world. Advertising has also developed its own historiography. Retro ads in the late 1990s, for instance, constitute historical self-reference. With computer techniques, images from 1950s commercials are incorporated into modern-day TV commercials, conveying a feeling for the supposedly simple, secure, good life of that era, and, at the same time, documenting the history of advertising. Providing a sense of order through historical continuity and recapitulated images, retro advertising is just one way in which advertisers adapt to change and need.

Now, not everyone in our culture thinks "neomaniacally." There are many who, as a matter of fact, react against this kind of outlook. But it is becoming symptomatic of increasingly larger sectors of the culture. And, in our view, advertising has become the discourse that reflects this cultural "symptomatology." Advertising has become a kind of cultural *meta-language*, textuality that sends out its messages instantly, effortlessly, sensorially. The magazine ad, for instance, can be viewed as contemporary *art* form combining the visual mode of representation (as do the fine arts) with the verbal one (as do the literary arts). It has become the "poetry" of contemporary society. Since ordinary people tend not to engage as a rule in "serious" reading or philosophical contemplation, it should come as little surprise to find that advertising has come forward to fill the need for poetry that exists in every human being.

No wonder, then, that advertising is being acknowledged as art more and more; having even its own category of prize at the Cannes film festival. Although we may superciliously be inclined to condemn its objectives, as an aesthetic-inducing experience we invariably enjoy it. Advertisements convince, please, and seduce. Advertising works aesthetically. And it is adaptive, constantly seeking out new forms of expression reflecting fluctuations in social trends and values. Not only, but its forms have even been adapted and coopted by mainstream artists and writers. Some pages of the contemporary writer Jean-Marie Gustave Le Clézio, for instance, reveal an amalgam of traditional literary expression and advertising styles and forms.

But there is a fundamental difference between the great works of art that all cultures identify as "saying something" about life and advertising. The goal of the great artists has always been to imbue our universal human experience with meaning and sense of purpose. The great works of visual art, the great dramas, the great music of *all* cultures, not just the Western one, are meant to transform the experience of human feelings and events into memorable works that transcend time and culture. Advertising, on the other hand, communicates nothing of any lasting or profound value, but trendy, "cool" attitudes and images. This new artistic vernacular constitutes a means aimed at grabbing the attention of a generation of individuals with seemingly reduced attention spans. Advertising is the art of the trivial, quickly becoming all too familiar and boring.

But we are of the opinion that the human spirit will prevail, and that our consumption-driven culture will eventually redefine and reconstitute itself. We also do not believe that people are victimized by advertising, as many critics would claim. Children and teenagers are more influenced to act by their families and by their peers than they are by media images. In our opinion, there is no causal link between television violence, for instance, and violence in society in general. Did television engender the wars fought throughout history, including the two devastating world wars in this last century? Did it spur Jack the Ripper to slash his victims to death? Was it responsible for all the horrendous crimes perpetrated in the name of religion, nationhood, and the like? It makes no sense whatsoever to think of television and advertising as instigators of specific kinds of aberrant behaviors. If that were so, then this principle would apply to all media, codes, and texts, including religious ones. What is more accurate to say is that the general *modus pensandi* and lifestyle models of our culture are reflected in the textuality of advertisements.

Even though we absorb the messages transmitted constantly by ads and commercials, and although these may have some unconscious effects on our behavior, we accept media images only if they suit our already-established preferences. If we complain about the shallowness of our television and advertising culture, we really have no one to blame but ourselves.

It is true, however, that advertising has probably contributed significantly to creating a desire for the lifestyles it portrays in other parts of the world. When asked about the stunning defeat of communism in eastern Europe, the Polish leader Lech Walesa was reported by the newspapers as saying that it all came from the television set, implying that television undermined the stability of the communist world's relatively poor and largely sheltered lifestyle with images of consumer delights seen in western programs and commercials. Different cultures have indeed been reshaped to the form and contents of television's textuality. Marshall McLuhan's phrase of the "global village" is still an appropriate one — television and advertising have shrunk the world and diminished the interval between thought and action.

Demographic surveys now show consistently that people spend more time in front of television sets than they do working, that watching TV is bringing about a gradual decline in reading, that television's textuality is leading to the demise of the nation state concept as ideas and images cross national boundaries daily through television channels. Television and advertising have triggered the twentieth century's own "Gutenberg revolution." But rather than homogenizing the world, it is our view that human diversity and ingenuity will lead to a greater variety in television programming and advertising and, therefore, in social textuality.

Thus, at the risk of sounding élitist, we believe that advertising will never be able to replace the traditional forms of artistic expression. These document humanity's search for spiritual meaning; their subtexts are open-ended and profound. Advertising, on the other hand, exploits our need for meaning trivially to enhance sales of a product. Many critics refer to the effects of advertising as *reification*, the process of encouraging people to identify their desires and needs with objects that can be bought and sold. Advertising seems no more just to advertise products, but to promote a way of life through reification. But we must not forget, as Leiss, Kline & Jhally (1990: 33) remind us, that: "Objections directed at advertisements, the industry, and its alleged social impacts are often indirect attacks on the so-called materialistic ethos of industrial society, or on capitalism in general as a social system; these are critiques of society masquerading as critiques of advertising."

The answer to the dilemma of advertising is not to be found in censorship or in any form of state control of media . Even if it were possible in a consumerist culture to control the contents of advertising, this would invariably prove to be counterproductive. The answer is, in our view, to become aware of the subtexts that ads and commercials generate with the help of semiotic analysis. When the human mind is aware of the hidden codes in texts, it will be better able to fend off the undesirable effects that such texts may cause. Semiotics can help to demystify advertising creativity.

Practical Activities
(for Advertisers, Marketers, and Media Students)

The following activities review the basic ideas and techniques introduced in previous chapters.

1. In line with the *Law of the Marketplace* suggest brand names, draw logos, and coin slogans or jingles for the following new products. Then provide the connotative chain(s) that you intend to generate with such strategies.

Product	Brand Name	Logo Design	Slogan/ Jingle	Connotative Chain(s)
car				
toothpaste				
laptop				
jeans				
nail polish				
toy				
cheese				
wine				
cell phone				
bra				
panty hose				

2. Now design and create several ads and/or commercials (using video equipment) that will deliver the signification system you have established for each product

3. You are given the task of redefining certain well-known products or services. You are to do this by changing the brand name and trade-

mark (if one exists) of each product or service, identifying the new system of connotations this is supposed to evokes and what kind of new textuality is to be used for it.

Product/Service	New Brand Name/Logo	New Conno- tations	Textuality
Drakkar Noir (cologne)			
Cadillac (automobile)			
Poison (perfume)			
State Farm (insurance)			
Marlboro (cigarettes)			
Purina Dog Chow			
Sunlight (detergent)			
Timex (watch)			
Bayer (aspirin)			
Wendy's (restaurant)			
BurgerKing (restaurant)			

4. Invent a new iconic, indexical, or symbolic brand name or logo for each existing product or service.

Product/ Service	New Iconic Brand Name/ Logo	New Indexical Brand Name/ Logo	New Symbolic Brand Name/ Logo
Camels (cigarettes)			
Fedex (courier)			
Tylenol (pain killer)			
Kellog's (cereal)			
Macintosh (computer)			
Marriott (hotel chain)			
American Express (credit card)			
Remy Martin (cognac)			
Fox Network (TV network)			
Memorex (cassette tape)			
Kodak (photography)			

5. Collect several print ads of baby products. Then fill in the following chart for each one:

Print Ad	Surface Level Nonverbal Signifiers Signifiers	Verbal	Textuality

6. Invent new slogans for the following brand name products according to the suggested verbal techniques:

Product/ Service	Metaphor	Alliteration	Formula	Imperative Verb Form
Camels (cigarettes)				
Fedex (courier)				
Tylenol (pain killer)				
Kellog's (cereal)				
Macintosh (computer)				
Marriott (hotel chain)				
American Express (credit card)				
Remy Martin (cognac)				
Fox Network (TV network)				
Memorex (cassette tape)				
Kodak (photography)				

7. Using Case 1 of chapter 4 as background, flesh out the product image of *Marlboro* cigarettes in contrast with *Camel's* cigarettes with a group of students in the class. Use the following techniques:

Collage	Imaginary World	Portrait Chinois	Picture Association	Slogan

8. Using the notion of connotative index, first carry out an analysis of a 10 ads for cigarettes. Then, ask a group of people (e.g. other students in the class) what each ad means to them. On that basis, assign a connotative index to each ad (high, mid, low):

9. Using the notion of semantic differential, set-up various scales to flesh out the connotations of well-known brands of the following products or services:

Honda Civic
Colgate's toothpaste
Allstate insurance
Geritol

Glossary

Advertising (from medieval Latin *advertere* "to direct one's attention to") any type or form of public announcement designed to promote the sale of specific commodities or services

Aesthesia the ability to experience sensation; in art appreciation it refers to the fact that our senses and feelings are stimulated by the art form

Alliteration the repetition of the initial consonant sounds or features of words

Anchorage Roland Barthes' notion that visual images in advertisements are polysemous (having many meanings) which are, however, *anchored* to particular meaning domains by specific interpreters

Brand image the creation of a personality for the product: i.e. the intentional creation of a product's name, packaging, price, and advertising style in order to create a recognizable personality for the product that is meant to appeal to specific consumers

Code the system in which signs are organized and which determines how they relate to each other to make meaningful texts

Communication social interaction through messages; the production and exchange of messages and meanings; the use of specific modes and media of sign-making to transmit feeling-states and messages

Connotation the extended or secondary meaning of a sign; the symbolic or mythic implications of certain signifiers

Connotative Chain chain of connotations associated with a product

Connotative Index degree of connotation associated with a product

Consumer advertising advertising directed toward the promotion of some product

Context	the environment (physical and social) in which signs are produced and messages generated
Decoding	the process of deciphering the message inherent in a code, text, etc.
Denotation	the primary meaning of a sign
Encoding	the process of putting a message together in terms of a specific code, text, etc.
Hermeneutics	the science or art of interpretation
Icon	a sign which has a direct (nonarbitrary) connection to a referent
Image	representation of a product or service in order to enhance its value aesthetically, socially, etc.
Index	a sign that has an existential connection to a referent (indicating that something or someone is located somewhere)
Interpretant	the process of adapting a sign's meaning in terms of personal and social experience
Intertextuality	the allusion within a text to some other text that the interpreter would have access to or knowledge of
Jingle	easy rhythmic and simple repetitions of sound, etc., as some poetry and music
Logo	distinctive company signature, trademark, colophon, motto, newspaper nameplate, etc.
Medium	the technical or physical means by which a message is transmitted
Message	any meaningful text produced with signs belonging to a specific code (or codes)
Metaphor	the signifying process by which two signifying domains *(A, B)* are connected *(A is B)* explicitly or implicitly
Myth	any story or narrative in early cultures that aims to explain the origin of something or someone

Mythology	the study of myths, or the creation of mythic connotations associated with some person or event
Narrative	something narrated, told or written, such as an account, story, tale, and even scientific theory
Object	a synonym for referent or signified; what is referred to in signification
Onomatopoeia	the iconic feature of words by which they represent a referent imitating one or several of its audio-oral properties (*drip, boom*, etc.)
Opposition	the process by which signs are differentiated through a minimal change in their form (signifier)
Paradigmatic	a structural relation between signs that keeps them distinct and therefore recognizable
Positioning	the placing or targeting of a product for the right people
Propaganda	any systematic dissemination of doctrines, views, etc. reflecting specific interests and ideologies (political, social, and so on)
Public relations	the activities and techniques used by organizations and individuals to establish favorable attitudes and responses in their behalf on the part of the general public or of special groups
Publicity	the craft of disseminating any information that concerns a person, group, event, or product through some form of public media
Referent	what is referred to (any object, being, idea, or event in the world)
Representamen	Charles S. Peirce's term for signifier
Representation	the process by which referents are designated by signs
Rhetoric	the study of the techniques used in all kinds of discourses, from common conversation to poetry
Semantic Differential	technique for fleshing our connotations from a product's image through contrasting scales

Semiology	Ferdinand de Saussure's term for the study of signs, now restricted, by and large, to the study of verbal signs
Semiosis	the comprehension and production of signs
Semiotics	the science or doctrine that studies signs
Sign	something that stands for something (someone) else in some capacity
Signification	the process of generating meaning through the use of signs
Signification System	system of connotative meanings established for a product or service through various techniques such as brand naming, creation of a logo, etc.
Signified	that part of a sign that is referred to; a synonym for referent and object
Signifier	that part of a sign that does the referring; the physical part of a sign
Slogan	catchword or catch phrase used to advertise a product
Structure	any repeatable or predictable aspect of signs, codes, and messages
Subtext	a text (message) implied by connotation within a text
Symbol	a sign that has an arbitrary (conventional) connection with a referent
Synesthesia	the evocation of one sense modality (e.g. vision) by means of some other (e.g. hearing); the juxtaposition of sense modalities (e.g. *loud colors*)
Syntagmatic	the structural relation that combines signs in code-dependent ways
Text	the actual message with its particular form and contents
Textuality	types of ads and commercials created to deliver the product's meaning
Trade advertising	advertising that is directed toward dealers and professionals through appropriate trade publications and media

Bibliography

The following bibliography constitutes our suggestions for more detailed reading on both advertising and semiotics.

Aaker, D. A. (1996). *Building Strong Brands*. New York: The Free Press.

Albion, M. and Farris, P. (1981). *The Advertising Controversy*. Boston: Auburn House.

Anderson, M. (1984). *Madison Avenue in Asia: Politics and Transnational Advertising*. Cranbury, N. J.: Associated University Presses.

Andren, G. L., Ericsson, L., Ohlsson, R., and Tännsjö, T. (1978). *Rhetoric and Ideology in Advertising*. Stockholm: AB Grafiska.

Atwan, R. (1979). *Edsels, Luckies and Frigidaires: Advertising the American Way*. New York: Dell.

Barnouw, E. (1978). *The Sponsor: Notes on a Modern Potentate*. Oxford: Oxford University Press.

Barthel, D. (1988). *Putting on Appearances: Gender and Advertising*. Philadelphia: Temple University Press.

Barthes, R. (1957). *Mythologies*. Paris: Seuil.

Barthes, R. (1967). *Système de la mode*. Paris: Seuil.

Barthes, R. (1977). *Image-Music-Text*. London: Fontana.

Bignell, J. (1997). *Media Semiotics: An Introduction*. Manchester: Manchester University Press.

Branston, G. and Stafford, R. (1999). *The Media Student's Book*. London: Routledge.

Brierley, S. (1995). *The Advertising Handbook*. London: Routledge.

Briggs, A. and Cobley, P. (1998) (eds.). *The Media: An Introduction*. Harlow: Longman.

Courtenoy, A. E. and Whipple, T. W. (1983). *Sex Stereotyping in Advertising*. Lexington, Mass.: Lexington Books.

Danesi, M. (1999). *Of Cigarettes, High Heels, and Other Interesting Things*. New York: St. Martin's.

Danesi, M. (2000). *An Encyclopedia Dictionary of Semiotics, Media, and Communication*. Toronto: University of Toronto Press.

Danesi, M. and Perron, P. (1999). *Analyzing Cultures*. Bloomington: Indiana University Press.

Danna, S. R. (1992). *Advertising and Popular Culture: Studies in Variety and Versatility*. Bowling Green, Ohio: Bowling Green State University Popular Press.

Driver, J. C. and Foxall, G. R. (1984). *Advertising Policy and Practice*. New York: Holt, Rinehart and Winston.

Dyer, G. (1982). *Advertising as Communication*. London: Routledge.

Eco, U. (1976). *A Theory of Semiotics*. Bloomington: Indiana University Press.

Ewen, S. (1976). *Captains of Consciousness*. New York: McGraw-Hill.

Ewen, S. (1988). *All Consuming Images*. New York: Basic.

Forceville, C. (1996). *Pictorial Metaphor in Advertising*. London: Routledge.

Fowles, L. (1976). *Mass Advertising as Social Forecast: A Method for Futures Research*. Westport: Greenwood Press.

Fox, S. (1984). *The Mirror Makers*. New York: William Morrow.

Frith, T. K. (1997). *Undressing the Ad: Reading Culture in Advertising*. New York: Peter Lang.

Goffman, E. (1979). *Gender Advertisements*. New York: Harper and Row.

Goldman, R. and Papson, S. (1996). *Sign Wars: The Cluttered Landscape of Advertising*. New York: The Guilford Press.

Harris, R. and Seldon, A. (1962). *Advertising and the Public*. London: André Deutsch.

Hawkes, T. (1977). *Structuralism and Semiotics*. Berkeley: University of California Press.

Heighton, E. and Cunningham, D. (1976). *Advertising in the Broadcast Media*. Belmont: Wadsworth.

Hayakawa, S. I. (1991). *Language in Thought and Action*, 5th ed. New York: Harcourt, Brace, Jovanovich.

Hindley, D. and Hindley, G. (1972). *Advertising in Victorian England*. London: Wayland.

Inglis, F. (1972). *The Imagery of Power: A Critique of Advertising*. London: Heinemann.

Jacobson, M. F. and Mazur, L. A. (1995). *Marketing Madness: A Survival Guide for a Consumer Society*. Boulder: Westview.

Jakobson, R. (1960). Linguistics and Poetics. In: T. A. Sebeok (ed.), *Style and Language*, pp. 34-45. Cambridge, Mass.: MIT Press.

Jhally, S. (1987). *The Codes of Advertising*. New York: St. Martin's Press.

Jones, J. P. (1999) (ed.). *How to Use Advertising to Build Strong Brands*. London: Sage.

Karmen, S. (1989). *Through the Jungle: The Art and Business of Making Music for Commercials*. New York: Billboard Books.

Key, W. B. (1989). *The Age of Manipulation*. New York: Holt.

Klein, N. (2000). *No Logo: Taking Aim at the brand Bullies*. Toronto: Alfred A. Knopf.

Lakoff, G. and Johnson, M. (1980). *Metaphors We Live By*. Chicago: University of Chicago Press.

Leiss, W., Kline, S. and Jhally, S. (1990). *Social Communication in Advertising: Persons, Products and Images of Well-Being*. Toronto: Nelson.

Leymore, V. (1975). *Hidden Myth: Structure and Symbolism in Advertising*. London: Heinemann.

Marchand, R. (1985). *Advertising the American Dream: Making the Way for Modernity, 1920-1940*. Berkeley: University of California Press.

McCracken, G. (1988). *Culture and Consumption*. Bloomington: Indiana University Press.

McLuhan, M. (1964). *Understanding Media*. London: Routledge and Kegan Paul.

Mittelart, A. (1991). *Advertising International*. London: Routledge.

Moog, C. (1990). *Are They Selling Her Lips? Advertising and Identity*. New York: Morrow.

Myers, G. (1994). *Words in Ads*. London: Arnold.

Nöth, W. (1990). *Handbook of Semiotics*. Bloomington: Indiana University Press.

O'Barr, W. M. (1994). *Culture and the Ad: Exploring Otherness in the World of Advertising*. Boulder: Westview.

O'Neill-Karch, Mariel (2000). Medievalism in Advertising as Value Transfer. In: J. Goering and F. Guardiani (eds.), *Medievalism: The Future of the Past*, pp. 11-31. Ottawa: Legas.

Ogden, C. K. and Richards, I. A. (1923). *The Meaning of Meaning*. London: Routledge and Kegan Paul.

Packard, V. (1957). *The Hidden Persuaders*. New York: McKay.

Pollay, R. W. (1979). *Information Sources in Advertising History*. Westport: Greenwood.

Pope, D. (1983). *The Making of Modern Advertising*. New York: Basic.

Presbrey, F. (1968). *The History and Development of Advertising*. Westport: Greenwood.

Rotzoll, K., Haefner, J. and Sandage, C. (1976). *Advertising and Society: Perspectives towards Understanding*. Columbus: Copywright Grid.

Schudson, M. (1984). *Advertising: The Uneasy Persuasion*. New York: Basic.

Seabrook, J. (2000). *Nobrow: The Culture of Marketing—The Marketing of Culture*. New York: Knopf.

Sebeok, T. A. (1991). *A Sign is Just a Sign*. Bloomington: Indiana University Press.

Sebeok, T. A. (1994). *Signs: An Introduction to Semiotics.* Toronto: University of Toronto Press.

Sinclair, J. (1987). *Images Incorporated: Advertising as Industry and Ideology.* Beckenham: Croom Helm.

Singer, B. (1986). *Advertising and Society.* Toronto: Addison-Wesley.

Sut, J. (1990). *The Codes of Advertising: Fetishism and the Political Economy of Meaning in the Consumer Society.* London: Routledge.

Thomas, F. (1997). *The Conquest of Cool.* Chicago: University of Chicago Press.

Umiker-Sebeok, J. (1987) (ed.). *Marketing Signs: New Directions in the Study of Signs for Sale.* Berlin: Mouton.

Vardar, N. (1992). *Global Advertising: Rhyme or Reason?* London: Chapman.

Vestergaard, T. and Schrøder, K. (1985). *The Language of Advertising.* London: Blackwell.

Wernick, A. (1991). *Promotional Culture: Advertising, Ideology, and Symbolic Expression.* London: Gage.

White, R. (1988). *Advertising: What it Is and How to Do It.* London: McGraw-Hill.

Williamson, J. (1985). *Decoding Advertisements: Ideology and Meaning in Advertising.* London: Marion Boyars.

Woodward, G. C. and Denton, R. E. (1988). *Persuasion and Influence in American Life.* Prospect Heights, Ill.: Waveland.